PLAygr...

Let your cre... ...y flow...

ode

limerick   haiku

rhyme

balla...

my poems

South & South East England
Edited by Lynsey Hawkins

Young**Writers**

First published in Great Britain in 2005 by:
Young Writers
Remus House
Coltsfoot Drive
Peterborough
PE2 9JX
Telephone: 01733 890066
Website: www.youngwriters.co.uk

SB ISBN 1 84602 099 9

Foreword

Young Writers was established in 1991 and has been passionately devoted to the promotion of reading and writing in children and young adults ever since. The quest continues today. Young Writers remains as committed to the fostering of burgeoning poetic and literary talent as ever.

This year's Young Writers competition has proven as vibrant and dynamic as ever and we are delighted to present a showcase of the best poetry from across the UK. Each poem has been carefully selected from a wealth of *Playground Poets* entries before ultimately being published in this, our thirteenth primary school poetry series.

Once again, we have been supremely impressed by the overall high quality of the entries we have received. The imagination, energy and creativity which has gone into each young writer's entry made choosing the best poems a challenging and often difficult but ultimately hugely rewarding task - the general high standard of the work submitted amply vindicating this opportunity to bring their poetry to a larger appreciative audience.

We sincerely hope you are pleased with our final selection and that you will enjoy *Playground Poets South & South East England* for many years to come.

Contents

Shannon Fox (8)	18
Brandon Bax (9)	19
Louise Withers (8)	19

Bedonwell Junior School, Belvedere

Leanne Wightwick (10)	20
Charlie Mills (9)	20
Sophie Ferguson (10)	21
Chloe Roche (9)	22
Liberty Coiley (9)	23
Jodie Barrett (10)	23
Ryan Evariste & Annabelle Owen (9)	24
Bradley Bryan (9)	24
Bethanie Short (9)	25
Emily Graham (8)	25
Alexander Ian Sanderson (9)	26
Daniel Grigg (9)	26
Aimee Livermore (9)	27
Charlie Withall (9)	27
Farrall Rose Williams (9)	28
Rheanne Bryant (9)	28
Tharshana Mahendrarajah (11)	29
Emma Louise Stafford (9)	29
Rebecca Smith (9)	30
Oliver Carlisle (9)	30
Lewis Winzar (9)	31
Jamie Williams (9)	31
Sonam Sadhra (10)	32
Molly England (11)	32
Lauren O'Brien (9)	33
Alice Young (10)	33
Sukvinder Sodhi (9)	34
Naomi Lee (7)	34
Dominic Chahal (8)	35
Deborah Mary Adebiyi (8)	05
James Sutton (10)	36
Shannon Scolding (8)	37
Molly Patterson (7)	37
Luke Parsons (9)	38

Bessemer Grange Primary School, London

Sam Baker (6)	38
Sydney Sinclair (7)	39
Michael Schick (6)	39
Wesley McDonald (7)	40
Joche Adde	40
Sam Atkinson (7)	41
Archie Barker (7)	41
Nabila Ahmed (10)	42
Kyus Holder (6)	42
Ruth Auld (11)	43
Wayne O'Brien (7)	43
John Napoleon Kuofie (11)	44
Sola Kusanu (7)	44
Maryja Cooper (11)	45
Kaine Broadhurst (7)	45
Adrienne Good (10)	46
Amaan Clarke (7)	46
Felicia Oduntan (10)	47
Daniel Diguilio (7)	47
Brittney Wallace (11)	47
James Adcock (11)	48
Dilys Akyeampong (10)	48

Collingwood School, Wallington

Jennifer Lucy Munden (10)	49
Alex Denning (10)	49
Rosie Maureen Molly Bain (11)	50
Oyinda Ayonrinde (10)	50
Krishan Sareen (9)	51
Ashok Menon (10)	51
Charlotte Brocklesby (10)	52
Daniel Bunting (11)	52
Emma Kenton (11)	53
Luke Hannigan (11)	53
Shilpa Suresh (10)	53
Jordan McGuinness (10)	54
Alexandra Elizabeth Reed (11)	54
Andrew Searle (11)	54
Jack Aguéra (10)	55
Matthew Brewer (10)	55

Harry Jones (9)	55
Fern Colepio (9)	56
Darren Mindham (10)	56
Tobi Adedayo Adeyemi (10)	56
James William Acquaye Nortey-Glover (10)	57
William Parsons (9)	57
Heather Filby (9)	57
Alfie Barnard Ford (9)	58
Eleanor Blackford (9)	58
Jordan Pini (9)	58
Will Evans (9)	59

Compton & Up Marden CE Primary School, Chichester

Alex Gillies (10)	59
Izzy Weston-Goodman (11)	59
Connor Cunningham (11)	60
Ellie Hoar (10)	60
Jack Coles (10) & Nathan Etherington (11)	61
Charlotte Mills (9)	61
Liam Dixon (10)	62
Charlotte Hill (9)	62
Luke Isom (9)	63
Thomas Woodcock (11) & Jack Mannings (9)	63
Charles Wade-Palmer (9)	64
Rory Watson (11) & Hugh Sawers (10)	65
Charlotte Beaman (10)	65

Crofton Anne Dale Junior School, Fareham

Abbie Fletcher (10)	66
Karly Higgs (9)	66
Hannah Miller (7)	67
Beth Sadler (9)	67
Sophie Coleman (11)	68
William Downham (9)	68
Daniel Fisher (11)	69
Laura Kingston (8)	69
Jessica Edney (8)	70
Isabelle Coleman (11)	70
Jasmine Kershaw (10)	71
Hannah Dewane (10)	71
Brooklyn Barber (10)	72

Kayleigh Fowler (10)	72
Madeleine Horst (10)	73
Josie Bagley (8)	73
Jordan Pearson (9)	74
Laura Macfarlane (9)	74
Kelly-Marie Holmes (8)	75
Alexandra McRobbie (8)	75
Poppy Saville (10)	76
Sam Goodsell (7)	76
Audrey Macleod (10)	77
Madeline Smith (10)	77
Sophie Charlotte Mary Keen (8)	78
Gemma Arnfield (9)	78
Alice Tucker (9)	79
Laura Green (11)	79
Jenna Andrews (9)	79

Egerton CE Primary School, Ashford

Emma Manning (10)	80
Gabriella Hasham (9)	80
Holly Smith (10)	81
Katie Hope (10)	81
Amy Heuch (10)	82
Ricky Ralph (10)	82
Beatrice Calver (10)	83
Alex Blowers (9)	83
Rebecca Amos (11)	84
Josh Deane (10)	84
Rachel Green (11)	85
Aaron Parr (10)	85
Ruby Gretton (10)	86
Sophie Major (11)	87
Seth Matthews (11)	87
Jennie Mackay (10)	88
Bryony Davison (10)	88

Four Elms Primary School, Edenbridge

Sophie Gardiner (9)	88
Christopher Allen (10)	89
Abigail Hamblin (9)	89
Annie Greenaway (10)	89

Madeleine Knapman (10)	90
Kirsty McGregor (9)	90
Ryan Johnson (10)	90
Danielle Jewhurst (11)	91
Andrew Gower Ballard (10)	91
Christy Mitchell (10)	91
Hannah Dewhirst (10)	92
Matthew Burton (11)	92

Harrison Primary School, Fareham

Connie Bloomfield (10)	93
Natasha Miller (10)	93
Jashan Solanki (9)	94
Thomas Kent (10)	94
Susan Dowell (10)	95
Vincent Cunning (10)	95
Benjamin Kissane (10)	96
Lara Gadsdon (10)	96
Sophie Hilliker (9) & Anna Davey-Evans (10)	97
Ryan Madden (10)	98
Alice Jones (9)	98
Rebecca Botham (9)	99
James Shayler (10)	99
Emma Rees (10)	99
Laura Colebrooke (9)	100
Holly Wheaton (9)	100
Bethan Gmitrowicz (10)	101
Jade Burrell (9)	101
Hannah Sharpe (9)	102
Daniel Edwards (10)	102
Jonathon Sheppard (9)	103
Fleur Gascoigne (10)	103
Ellen McDonald (9)	103
Lauren Taylor (9)	104
Freya Bowes (9)	104
Maria Roberson (9)	105
Alice Frampton (9)	105
Peter Kovacs (10)	105
Anna Harriman (9)	106
Abigail Fifield (9)	106
Chloe Llowarch 10)	106

Rachel Martin (10)	125
Luke Jackson (10)	125
Patrick Redmond (10)	126
Lewis McCormack (10)	126
Heather Martin (10)	127
Ben Jones (10)	127
Christopher Herbert (10)	128

Mereworth CP School, Mereworth

Lily Johnson (10)	129
Tom Cuttle (11)	129
Hannah Bond (10)	130
George Campbell (10)	131
Melanie Cuddon (10)	132
Ben Edmonds (10)	133
Jessica Calderwood (10)	134
Sarah Loines (10)	135
Zoe Moore (11)	135
Lauren Smith (10)	136
William Ashworth (11)	137
Heidi Beaven (10)	138
Abigail McCarthy (10)	138
Laura Edmonds (10)	139
Holly Burgess (11)	140
Rebecca Leong (10)	141
Lauren Hare (10)	142
George Tye (10)	143
Rebecca Sampson (10)	144
Christopher Allen (11)	145
Georgia Dallas (10)	146
Sian Fenn (10)	147
Hollie Dixson (10)	148
Ryan Pass (11)	149
Nathan Kiddie (10)	150
George Farrington (10)	151
Lorna Crease (10)	152

Merlin Primary School, Bromley

Claire Birchall (11)	152
Amber Simmonds (11)	153
Danielle Campion (11)	153

Selin Ozkosar (10)   154
Kieran Hopkins (10)   154
Sammie Delany (11)   155
Luke O'Toole   155
Adem Hassan (10)   155

Merton Court School, Sidcup
Joe Taylor (10)   156
Joshua White (10)   156
Sam Lateo (10)   157
Bethan Warman (10)   158
Ellis Rose Crawshaw (10)   158
Sam Griffin-Beat (11)   159
Charlee Brace-Bywater (10)   160
Katerina Charalambous (11)   160
Andrew Clode (10)   161
Michael Currans (11)   162
Vincent Lam (10)   163
Alyssa Matharu (11)   164
Jamie-Leigh O'Reilly (10)   165
Henry Pyle (10)   166
Harpiar Seehra (10)   167
Sophie Taylor-Jones (10)   168
Lauren Thomas (11)   169
Edward Wallis (10)   170
Joseph Ives (10)   171
Joseph Ansell (10)   171
Yasmin Mustafa (11)   172

Monega Primary School, London
Imtiyaz Zaman (10)   172
Aysha Patel (10)   173
Pooja Samji (10)   174
Sachin Dabasia (11)   174
Johura Khatun (11)   175
Sonyea Uddin (11)   175
Kaisha Mandalia (10)   176
Anzal Javaid (11)   177
Sachin Patel (10)   177
Rimsha Iqbal (10)   178
Harris Rehman (11)   178

Sunita Luggah (10)	179
Fariha Rahman (11)	179
Humna Iqbal (9)	180
Mamta Vaiyata (10)	181

Oval Primary School, Croydon
Huon Vassie (9)	181
Paul Anderson (9)	182
Matthew Anderson (8)	182

St Joseph's Convent School, London
Hannah Edmundson (9)	183
Grace McAuliffe (9)	183
Annabelle Juffs (9)	184
Tanyia Ahmed (9)	185
Julide Ayger (9)	185
Jessica Anthony (9)	186
Philippa Archibald (10)	186
Annabeth Ravensdale (9)	187
Loanna Katana (9)	188
Joanna Mall (9)	188
Nicole Ashraf (10)	189
Lily Atherton (10)	189
Louise Bradbury (10)	190
Kate Roberts (9)	191
Trisha Seeromben (9)	192
Terimelda Kyomuhendo (9)	192
Emma Flynn (10)	193
Emily Wong (9)	194
Claudia Holmes (10)	195
Olivia Collins (9)	196
Thandiwe Adeshiyan (9)	197
Lucinda Dawson (10)	198

St Luke's Primary School, London
Courtney Francis (10)	198
Bipul Deb (11)	199
Jonathan Bradford (11)	199
Zack Karhani (11)	200
Burak Gunduz (11)	200

Shuhala Ahad (11)	201
Harry Edwards (10)	201
Tyrus Williams (11)	202
Tosin Akande (10)	202
Pippa Thirkettle (11)	203
Nana Abeyie (10)	203
Mumin Choudouhry (11)	204
Sam Bassett (10)	204
Luisa Avery (11)	205
Stacy Humphries (10)	205
Ayat Abdurahman (10)	205
Bria Patel (11)	206
Janatara Ahmed (10)	206

Stamford Hill Primary School, London

Rushane McGhie (10)	207
Lisa Thi Tran (10)	207
Shayo Bayo-Tofowomo (10)	208
Ronell Hatto (11)	208
Raine Mondesir-Payne (11)	209

Stoke Community School, Rochester

Mazie Mason (11)	209
Sophie Ross (11)	210
Dean Bailey (12)	210
Danielle Coe (9)	211
Emily Williams (9)	211
Arri Wall (12)	212
Chloe Cocker (12)	212
Eloise Henderson (10)	213
Leanne Button (12)	213
Charles Harris (12)	214
Ashley Wall (9)	214
Tiana Kingsnorth (9)	215
Amanda Jacobs (12)	215
Aimee Draper (11)	216
Rebecca Gapper (10)	216
Chloe Stroud (11)	217
Michelle Toland (11)	217
Declan Kingsley (9)	218
Kayleigh Rousell (11)	218

Harry Hilton (10)	219
Alice Barrett (11)	219
Blair Robb (10)	220
Lewis Ilsley (9)	220
James Blown (11)	221
Sean Turner (9)	221

West Borough Primary School, Maidstone

Bethany Martin (9)	222
Ashleigh Briggs (9)	223
Darshna Rajesh Nemane (10)	223
Summer Leagas (9)	224
Rianne Hobbs (10)	224
Jodie Hall (10)	225
Betony Dubock (8)	225
Ryan Noon (9)	226
Charlotte Livingstone (11)	226
Rosie Judge (11)	227
Bryony Curtis (8)	227
Kathleen Boakes (11)	228
Mark Skinner (11)	228
Hayley Nyman (8)	229
Kimberley Grace Mercer (9)	229
Tom Tucker (8)	229
Jade Bunyan-Wilding (11)	230
Bradley J Marchant (10)	230
Zoe Smith (11)	230
Eden Selway (11)	231
Ella Selway (7)	231
Louise Paine (8)	231
Emilia Page (9)	232
Maxwell Whiting (9)	232
Hannah Daly (9)	233
Luke Osina (9)	233
Lucy Kelly (10)	234
Miriam Lebrette (11)	234
Marcus Edwards (10)	235
Geetha Thaninathan (9)	235
Lacie Shepherd (8)	235
Kaye-Dee Evanson (11)	236
Martha La Rosa-Butler (7)	236

The Poems

Untitled

Shopping is believing
what you buy is who you are,
So stop and think what you're buying
before you get in your car.

Think about the animals,
think about their lives.
Think about the chickens,
have they ever seen the light?

Shopping is believing
what you buy is who you are,
So stop and think what you're buying,
it could take you far.

Do you need sheepskin?
Do you need leather?
Do you need horse glue,
which keeps your books together?

Shopping is believing
what you buy is who you are.
So stop and think what you're buying
before you get in your car.

Do you buy bananas
just because they're cheap?
Buy Fair Trade,
and help people to their feet.

You don't have to listen,
but keep in the back of your head.
What you eat is who you are -
and don't forget!

Believe in yourself!

Puja Mehta & Rosie Shoop

Happy Is When . . .

Happy is when I get a pocket money rise
Happy is when it's Saturday and you get to have a lie in
Happy is when you're on second period, break is next
The happiest thing out of all these things is when it's night-time
And your mum tucks you in bed and gives you a goodnight kiss.

Sonam Sidhu (11)

The Sea

The sea is blue,
The sea is wide,
The sea moves left and right.
The waves ride high and low,
The waves ride high and low.
Oh I wish I was a dolphin,
Swimming in the sea.

Georgia Hylands (8)
Beaufort Primary School, Woking

Wolves

Wolves howl at the moon,
like they're saying, 'Toodle-oo!'
Wolves travel in packs
you never know, they might strike back.
Wolves eat meat
they don't eat sweets,
so if you hear a wolf
don't forget to go . . .
'Howwwwwwwl!'

Leayah Smith (9)
Beaufort Primary School, Woking

The Tudors

The Tudor times were so surreal
they came and went and yet still
we remember the many kings and queens
who lived and breathed through
hard times, it seems.

Henry VIII, he was a cruel king
who had many wives in the hope
they would bring an heir to the throne
to continue the reign,
sadly his efforts were all in vain.

Unlike his father Henry VII,
who was known to be extremely pleasant
he conquered the Battle of Bosworth successfully
that made him King of England, eventually!

It was he who discovered the Tudor times
where due to poverty, there were many crimes.

Omar Khan (9)
Beaufort Primary School, Woking

My Dog

My little dog is called Holly,
She takes a sneaky lick,
She is so sweet and lovely.
I throw a ball for her,
She runs and jumps
And catches it and brings it
Straight back to me.

Matt Stevens (9)
Beaufort Primary School, Woking

Seven Ways Of Looking At Winter

Winter,
Snowflakes falling faster
and faster, like the horrible rain.

Winter,
Children playing out in the
snow, making snowballs.

Winter,
Children making snowmen,
like the tall tree.

Winter,
Frozen lakes, like the icy
broken tap.

Winter,
People walking slower
and slower, like the
freezing cat.

Winter,
Snowflakes hanging down
people's roofs.

Winter,
Adults cooking
Christmas dinner.

Megan Brooke (7)
Beaufort Primary School, Woking

Fireworks With A Bang!

I'm really excited,
It's fireworks tonight.
The whizzing and popping
And hot dogs, all night.
My favourite firework
Is the great ruby-red.
Oh, here it comes,
Bang!

I'd much rather be outside
With my friends
Than sitting inside, looking out.

Ashley Williams (8)
Beaufort Primary School, Woking

Disneyland

D isneyland is really fun,
I n Disneyland there are lots of rides.
S creaming children wait their turn,
N ervously, people stand in the line.
E very day there are parades and shows.
Y oung children are very excited.
L ots of candyfloss gets handed out,
A ll the characters walk around.
N ans and grandads enjoy themselves as well,
D isneyland is a great place to go!

Liam Brabrook (8)
Beaufort Primary School, Woking

Secret Agents

S ecret agents, everywhere. Here, there, anywhere,
E very spy in the street and they don't care who they meet.
C oming to get our information.
R eturning it to their own nation.
E nemy forces must be found,
T hey creep about and make no sound.

A sking questions, telling lies,
G etting shot and someone dies.
E very secret mission means
N eutralising all our fiends.
T o make my foes think I'm a friend,
S hall bring this project to an end.

Lee Jones (9)
Beaufort Primary School, Woking

Anger

Anger is like a drum pounding through my head,
Anger is like a boulder rolling down a huge steep hill.
Anger is like fire on a blood-red stick,
Anger is like thunder, flickering in the sky.
Anger is like sandpaper, scraping on your hand,
Anger is like lightning, flashing through my eyes,
Anger is like water rushing around my head.
Anger, anger, anger!

I hate being angry.

Ash Ould-Dada (8)
Beaufort Primary School, Woking

Friends

Friends are there when you're down,
They know you're upset when you frown.

They're funny and cool,
They would look after you when you're a fool.

They always help you through the bad,
They would listen to you and never get mad.

That is why friends were made,
One of the best things God made!

They also make you not afraid,
But when you fall out, friendship won't fade.

You always make up without a doubt,
Friends will always take you out.

That's why we need friends.

Natalie Jane Maher (9)
Beaufort Primary School, Woking

Love

Love makes you feel warm,
One true kiss on a romantic date.
Valentine's Day brings love into the air,
We all need someone to love.

Love smells like dozens of roses,
Love tastes as sweet as sugar.
Love is comforting when you have
Someone beside you . . .

We all need someone to love.

Charlotte Cann (9)
Beaufort Primary School, Woking

Football

How I love football,
It's the greatest sport,
Chelsea, Man United and Liverpool
Are a few of the teams that we support.

Those in the know call it
The 'beautiful game',
But wherever it's played
It's always the same.

Pelé, Maradona and Ronaldo,
Are some of the greatest players.
I love all their skills,
Unless they play for Arsenal, especially Reyes.

My favourite team is Chelsea,
They are better than the rest.
Other teams are good
But Chelsea are the best.

Ben Smith (9)
Beaufort Primary School, Woking

Rainbows

Rainbows, rainbows
Orange, red and green
If you don't believe me
Find the end and see.
Rainbows, rainbows
Everlasting rainbows.

Rainbows are yellow
Rainbows are pink
Rainbows are all the colours
You can think!

Grace Stanley (9)
Beaufort Primary School, Woking

Carp

I'm the fattest in the lake,
And no one can ever eat me.
I always eat and always get caught,
And never live in the sea.

Anglers always beat me
Because I am so dumb,
I can't even see
The answer to a sum.

I always eat boilies,
Most of the time on a hook,
They taste really nice
And I like the way they look.

Everyone tries to catch me,
Because I weigh so much.
That's the end of my poem,
Thank you very much.

Connor Maltby (9)
Beaufort Primary School, Woking

Hallowe'en

Children walking in the street,
Going into houses to trick or treat.

Witches flying on their broom,
Off they go, off they zoom.

Dracula in his scary tomb,
Saying, 'Welcome to the tomb of doom!'

Werewolves dancing in the night,
So now they will never give you a fright.

Rebecca Ly (9)
Beaufort Primary School, Woking

Football

Refs make wrong decisions,
In all of the divisions.
Linesmen run down the wing,
Crowds chant and sing.

Tottenham have been cheated,
Then it all got heated.
Managers debate the offside rule,
Before and after they've kicked a ball.

Players fined for elbowing,
Famous players have money and bling.
Random drug tests catch players out,
Managers and captains rave and shout.

The FA says what's on and what's not,
Players play in weather, cold and hot.
Transfer windows are great,
You could catch up with an old mate!

The best teams are Chelsea, Arsenal and Real Madrid,
Rich people try and take over clubs with bids.
Football is the best sport
It's one of a kind.

Craig Harrison (9)
Beaufort Primary School, Woking

My Tiger

My tiger, he creeps all around, softly on the ground.
He snuggles up, in bed we lie,
Down with our heads,
Together we have a good sleep.
In the morning we will creep,
'Cause my mum doesn't know he is here,
If she did, it would give her a scare.

Jade Bystram (9)
Beaufort Primary School, Woking

My Dad's Scared Of Frogs

My dad's six foot tall,
He's as broad as a house
With muscles all over
But he's as scared as a mouse.

Once I was clearing out my nan's pond,
It was a really clear day,
I wanted to show him a frog
But then he just ran away.

I went fishing once,
It was just me and my dad
A watery fat toad hopped up
And dad went mad.

He just can't help it,
He was born like that,
But when it comes to frogs,
He's a big scaredy-cat!

Sam Hopper (9)
Beaufort Primary School, Woking

Fairies

At the bottom of my garden
Among the roses there
Sat a group of fairies
With long golden hair.

I watched them all night and day
I watched them dance
I watched them play
I watched them fly, fly away.

Jessica Watkins (9)
Beaufort Primary School, Woking

Mice

Are you sure you like mice?
They're not very nice
They could give you a fright
A nibble or a bite.

Their black bulging eyes
Can cause a surprise
Their reflective white teeth
Can bite through beef.

Some coats are white
Which are shiny and bright
Their little red noses
Are the colour of roses.

Have you changed your mind?
Do you think mice are kind?
Are you sure you like mice?
I told you, they're not nice!

Thomas Clapton (10)
Beaufort Primary School, Woking

Winter

Winter's here, winter's back
The snow has come
The snow is back
Covering our houses
Covering our town
The snow is everywhere
All over the ground
Snowflakes falling like crystals gleaming
They look so pretty, they look so beaming
Snow is falling everywhere
When I go outside it gets in my hair
Winter's back, winter's here
So enjoy it now, before it disappears.

Sabrina Ahmed (10)
Beaufort Primary School, Woking

Angry

I get angry when people have no respect for me
Why don't they care for thee?
When I go to school
They treat me like a fool
They laugh at me if I get a question wrong
I wish I was big and strong
And when school ends
I meet my friends
I tried to hurt them
But I wasn't too certain
Except it was the other way round
But I tried not to make any sound
I tried to run away
But they wouldn't stay
I went to tell the staff
But it was time to go into class
Instead I told Mr Hay
But he wouldn't listen, he had to go away.

Jason Foskett (9)
Beaufort Primary School, Woking

Kangaroos

Kangaroos bounce all day and bounce all night
Don't be afraid, they don't bite.
They feed so gently from your hand
And frolic in the sand.

The little joeys love their mums
They start in pouches in their tums.
The daddies sometimes go and fight
And kick-box with all their might.

Jamie Rest (9)
Beaufort Primary School, Woking

Cats

Monty is a stripy cat,
Snowball is brown and white.
They play together.
Nicky and I play fairy cats.
We choose which cat to be.
The cat jumps high then falls.
Henry is a brown cat,
Smoky is half-brown and black.
They search for their friends.
Scat cat is friendly,
Nibbly is shy,
Nip is cute,
Chip is crazy and eats a lot.
Whisper likes to hide from me.
Congo likes kung fu.
Chicky pecks a lot.
Scorch is kind.

Andrew Widdicombe (9)
Beaufort Primary School, Woking

Fantasy Fireworks

Fireworks are colourful, fireworks are bright
I could stand here and watch them all night.
Some are pink, some are yellow.
Some go *bang* and some say hello.
Some are red, some blue, most of them are new.
We stand there watching them, mouth open wide
And we shout, 'It's cold, let's go inside!'
Fireworks are pretty, fireworks are fun.
I'm standing here with my chocolate bun.

Ellen Savage (9)
Beaufort Primary School, Woking

Annoying Games

Don't these games just get on your nerves?
Battle here -
Then you have to drive around a pier.
Nuts, I was turned to stone in a bin,
I lost in the race because I drove over a pin.
Nooooo! I was a second too slow,
Now my car won't go.
They just burned my men,
What the? I'm being eaten by a killer hen!
Die, die, you enemies,
Fall back! They're throwing peas.
Now I'm off to outer space,
Nuts, I lost: our planet was taken by the alien race.
Now that concludes my little rhyme,
For I have expired the time.

Stephen Robinson (9)
Beaufort Primary School, Woking

Summer

S un is out and it's time to play
U nder the cool water in the pool
M um takes us to the hot warm beaches
M e and my brother play outside
E ating a picnic in the park on a hot day
R acing with my brother into the soft sea.

Hannah Lay (8)
Beaufort Primary School, Woking

Seven Ways Of Looking At Winter

Winter,
A lovely set of snow like an ice cube.

Winter,
with icicles that hang like frozen tears.

Winter,
Like an icy piece of paper.

Winter,
Like a massive ice rink all over the floor.

Winter,
Snowy as Lapland.

Winter,
As warm as a cat when I'm indoors.

Winter,
Like holly climbing up your window.

Anna Harrison (7)
Beaufort Primary School, Woking

King Of The Jungle

A terrifying roar echoes through the jungle.
The trees bend and shake from the soundwaves.
He's the bravest creature on Earth,
But not as brave as Superman.

He's yellow like the shining sun,
He's huge like a bus.
He runs as fast as an express train.

Who is it?
Why it's the magnificent lion.
The king of the jungle.
The mightiest cat in the world.

Omar Ismail (8)
Beaufort Primary School, Woking

Seven Ways Of Looking At Winter

Winter,
Is the chilliest season of the year.

Winter,
Is when you sit next to the fire.

Winter,
Snowball fights.

Winter,
Very chilly.

Winter,
You have colds and runny noses.

Winter,
Icy lakes.

Winter,
Fir trees.

Connor Pink (8)
Beaufort Primary School, Woking

My Dog Rory

My dog is scruffy and really fluffy!
My dog likes to have a walk
My dog loves his treats!
My dog Rory is very playful
My dog is scared of leaves!
But I love my dog most of all
Because he is so sweet!

Nichola Moore (9)
Beaufort Primary School, Woking

Dolphins

Dolphins are cute
Dolphins are kind
Dolphins can save your life

Dolphins can wriggle their tail left and right
Dolphins can wriggle in the sea very fast, *swoosh!*
Dolphins are the best things around here.

Dolphins are cute
Dolphins are kind
Dolphins can save your life

Dolphins are great fun
Dolphins like the sea
They're the best thing.

Dolphins are cute
Dolphins are kind
Dolphins are the best thing!

Misbah Hussain (9)
Beaufort Primary School, Woking

My Cat

Cats are cuddly,
Cats are cute.
Cats are soft,
I love them lots.

Shannon Fox (8)
Beaufort Primary School, Woking

Omaha Beach

Here I am on my way to my death.
I pray to God I see my wife.
30 seconds till I meet my doom and die.
I'm ready to fight to keep my country safe.
I feel like I am going to die.
My friend is beside me in terror.
We begin to run up the beach
When he is shot, I'm on my own.
Two days later I reach the city.
Feeling sad, feeling low.
People's homes destroyed, people's lives gone.
Why do we do this? It's not right!

Brandon Bax (9)
Beaufort Primary School, Woking

Football

My dream is to be a footballer, a footballer it is,
Just thinking about it, it makes me feel weird.
It's all the powerful kicking
All the fast running,
All the fantastic saving.
All the screeching crowds and the jumping ball.
It's just my dream to be a footballer,
a footballer it is!

Louise Withers (8)
Beaufort Primary School, Woking

Ocean Waves

Little mermaid in the sea, will you come and play with me?
I love your tail, pink and red, and the golden hairs upon your head.
I think you swim so gracefully, above and among the seaweed.
You play with seahorses, you play with the rays,
You play with a different fish, every day.
So can I come and play with you, down in the ocean, ocean blue?

Little oyster your name is Earl, in one hundred years you'll
Make a pearl.
You live in amongst seaweed and coral, you don't fuss,
You don't quarrel.
You live your life so peacefully, even though you're 83.
I hope you make a pearl for me, as you live your life in the sea.

Starfish, starfish in the sea, your colour is so orangy,
You live in the sea, you live in the sky, you brighten the Earth
All through the night.

Jellyfish, jellyfish, you sting with silver strands,
You don't have arms, you don't have hands.

Mister Crabby Crabson, walking down the beach,
Cockle shells cackle and seagulls screech.

This is my poem about under the sea,
I hope you enjoyed it as much as me.

Leanne Wightwick (10)
Bedonwell Junior School, Belvedere

Winter

Winter is oh so very cold
You have to be extremely bold
To go and play in the snow
And make a great big ball to throw
The wind howls all day long
And blows the leaves around, so strong
So stay indoors and keep yourself warm
And keep out of the way of that great big storm.

Charlie Mills (9)
Bedonwell Junior School, Belvedere

The Bird Mother

See the birds
Dark and fair,
I wonder how
They all got there?
For the beautiful creatures
In all their glory,
Have all heard
This same old story.
Of the bird mother
Who came to see
How beautiful
The Earth could be.
If dancing creatures
Ruled the land
Nesting on treetops
Squawking in sands.
And so
The very first bird was made,
But for that
The Earth Mother surely paid.
For every beak would cost a pebble
And every wing a pie,
But as she watched a fox pass by
A tear came to her eye.
Her creatures would suffer,
And that was no lie,
And that very day
In all her dismay,
She laid down and died.

Sophie Ferguson (10)
Bedonwell Junior School, Belvedere

My Magnificent Wolf

My wolf is rich silver,
Like a sword's blade spearing the enemy.
Silver like the midnight stars, glowing
Silver like diamonds with the sun shining down on them.

His eyes light up like bright spotlights
Shining through the forest.
My wolf is dark, like a pitch-black room
Which hadn't been open for years.

He is good and evil mixed together,
Half of him is dark, like the black stripes
On a zebra.
Half of him is light like the golden sunshine,
His back is fluffy like Mr Tibbles' coat.
His jaw is full of razor-sharp teeth
That can chew through anything.
His white spot in the centre of his head
Stands out like a very sore thumb.
He resembles the Queen's gold and silver.

I will lay my life down for you, my wolf.
Eat, my fluffy friend, eat!
I will protect you, I will protect you.
I will never forget you
I hope you never forget *me!*

Chloe Roche (9)
Bedonwell Junior School, Belvedere

My Magnificent Cheetah

My cheetah is orange like the evening sun,
Orange like a tan in the summer morning.
Orange like juice being poured into a glass.

He is as fast as a shooting star,
His shoulders go up and down
While you quiver with fear.
He roars like a volcano erupting,
He is night and day
The summer and winter.
He is your air.
I will give my life to save yours.
If poachers come, I shall back them off
With my spear.
Run around, run.
Be free.
Run with me.

Liberty Coiley (9)
Bedonwell Junior School, Belvedere

Springtime

The grass is jewelled with droplets of rain,
It's the beginning of springtime once again
I watched the flowers start to grow
I heard the whistle of the winds blow
The animals came out of their holes
The rabbits, the badgers and the moles
Birds and bees flying high in the sky
If you look up, you'll see them pass by.

Jodie Barrett (10)
Bedonwell Junior School, Belvedere

My Magnificent Leopard

My leopard is spotty like a Dalmatian
Walking in the sunset,
Yellow like the sunset.
Yellow like the reflection of the sunshine.
It sprints through the unwinding grass,
It is half sunshine and darkness.
Its teeth are razor-sharp like
A glistening dagger.
Its white chin is like snow, floating
In the winter breeze,
Its ears are as pointed as the edge of a square.

I will look after you whatever happens,
And I will sacrifice myself if needed.
I will protect you from enemies and hunters,
You are my leopard and I will protect you
Until I die.

Ryan Evariste & Annabelle Owen (9)
Bedonwell Junior School, Belvedere

My Magnificent Dingo

My magnificent dingo is gold like the sun,
Gold like the blistering desert.
Gold like the glowing goldfish.
My dingo howls like the wolf at a full moon,
He leaps like a kangaroo racing from his enemies.
He runs like a leopard, full speed ahead.
I will protect you from danger,
This peak is yours now.

Bradley Bryan (9)
Bedonwell Junior School, Belvedere

Dragon's Race

Oh dragon, dragon,
You're as massive as a wagon.
Your teeth are as sharp as razors,
Your eyes look like fierce red lasers.
The daring dragon had a race,
Even though it was like a maze.
His spiky tail swished,
But by the time he got there . . .
Dinner was dished.
His ears moved, swaying when he did,
But his purple scales without any doubt, slid!
He breathed out impressive orange flames,
Even then they called him names.
Oh dragon, you came fifth,
Or are you just a myth?

Bethanie Short (9)
Bedonwell Junior School, Belvedere

Me

My name is Emily and I'm so heavenly,
My surname is Graham and I'm always causing mayhem!
You might see me around places,
I'm the one with glasses.
I love to dance, I love to sing
I love to wear my bling, bling.
Bedonwell is my school,
I love it, it's so cool.
That's me, Emily.

Emily Graham (8)
Bedonwell Junior School, Belvedere

My Magnificent Leopard

My leopard is orange like the blazing sun,
Orange like the desert in Africa
Orange like a deadly frog.
He leaps like a fish, heading for his prey
In the sky.
My leopard is light, like the volcano ashes,
He is like the lord of the sun.
Half of him is a black portal,
Half of him is as light as Heaven.
His black shines like sun on gold.

I will water him at the river,
With my spear I will kill food,
Let them feed on other things.
The food belongs to me and my leopard.
Eat, my leopard, from the crops,
I am here to guard you with my spear.

Alexander Ian Sanderson (9)
Bedonwell Junior School, Belvedere

My Magnificent Leopard

My leopard,
He is like the morning sun
His black spots shimmer like midnight,
His eyes flicker in the blackness of the jungle.

His roar sounds like the stamping of an elephant,
He travels through the deep green bushes of the jungle.
He is good on the inside
And bad on the outside,
And I will look after him for the rest of my life,
And I will risk my life for him.
Drink, drink my pet, don't ever be thirsty.

Daniel Grigg (9)
Bedonwell Junior School, Belvedere

My Magnificent Leopard

My leopard is like the morning sun
His black spots shimmer like midnight.
His eyes flicker in the blackness of the jungle.

His roar sounds like a stomp of an elephant
He travels through the deep green bushes
Of the jungle.

He is good on the inside and
Bad on the outside.

I will look after him and
I will risk my life for him.
Drink my pet, drink my pet,
Don't ever be sad.

Aimee Livermore (9)
Bedonwell Junior School, Belvedere

My Magnificent Tiger

My tiger is orange like the sun beating down on the tiger,
Dark like the night sky.
The eyes are like the smiling moon on the water.
It moves, it is stalking up on its prey.
Orange and black is like good and bad fighting.
I will peck you with my iron whip.
Eat, my tiger, eat.

Charlie Withall (9)
Bedonwell Junior School, Belvedere

My Magnificent Leopard

My leopard is orange, like a bonfire,
Orange like magnificent gold, gleaming,
Orange like the deserts.
His roar is like a volcano erupting
And falling to the ground.
My leopard is bright like the sun setting,
He is day and night.
Half of him is like sunshine,
Half of him is darkness.
His back shines like the darkness of the stars.
His eyes are gazing away.
He resembles his master.
I will look after him wherever he goes,
I shall protect him in every way.
Let them water their herds somewhere else,
This river belongs to me and my leopard.
Drink, my sweet leopard from this river
I am here to guard you every day I live.

Farrall Rose Williams (9)
Bedonwell Junior School, Belvedere

My Magnificent Cheetah

My cheetah is as orange as the blazing sun,
Orange like a fire in the midnight sky,
Orange like a parrot's beak.
He runs as fast as a car in a race.
My cheetah is good and evil.
Half of him is evil from the depths of Hell,
Half of him is good, like an angel.
His eyes glow like headlamps in the pitch-black sky.

I will let you run down the riverbank,
I will drive any enemies away.
The riverbank belongs to me and you.

Run my cheetah, run. I am here to guard you.

Rheanne Bryant (9)
Bedonwell Junior School, Belvedere

The Disaster . . .

The Sri Lankans rested for two years
After the two decimal fights here!
But who thought that a disaster was near
At the end of a great year?
Tsunami, the name I hear
Of the disaster which the world
Couldn't bear.
Thousands dead, wounded and missing are here.
The disaster started in Sumatra,
And went up to Somalia for its share!
Many helped the agonised, with love and care.
Ill treatment is now very, very rare.
After the disaster, unkindness has gone into thin air!
We must try to forget this nightmare,
For all is for good and God is everywhere.

Tharshana Mahendrarajah (11)
Bedonwell Junior School, Belvedere

My Magnificent Rhino

My rhino is sparkly grey like a sapphire
Sparkling in the moonlight
Grey like a magnificent dark night sky
Creeping amongst the clouds
Green like a thunderbolt heading towards me.
He moves like a tremendous cheetah,
Searching for his prey.
My rhino is the most bold, magnificent creature
Ever to roam the land.
I will protect you even if my life depends on it.
Eat, my rhino, for I am here for you.

Emma Louise Stafford (9)
Bedonwell Junior School, Belvedere

My Magnificent Tiger

My magnificent tiger is orange
Like the blazing sun,
In the orange sky.
Orange like the blistering desert,
Orange like a dead leaf, lying
Flat on the ground
Its roar is like an ear-splitting noise,
Like a nail going down a blackboard.
It moves as soft as passing ghosts,
Half of him is dark, like the midnight sky,
And the other is light, like the rising sun.

His eyes are as sharp as a spear,
I will feed him at my tent
With my spear.
I will barge all of my enemies away.
This is my tent and they can go and find their own.
This place belongs to me
                              and
                          my
                              tiger!

Rebecca Smith (9)
Bedonwell Junior School, Belvedere

My Magnificent Tiger

My tiger is orange, like the sun beating down on the tiger,
Dark like the night sky.
The eyes, like the shining moon on the water.
It moves like it's stalking its prey.
It's orange and black,
Like good and bad fighting.
I will protect you with my whip,
Eat my tiger, I will protect you with my whip.

Oliver Carlisle (9)
Bedonwell Junior School, Belvedere

My Magnificent Snake

My snake is multicoloured like the parrot
Multicoloured with orange, yellow, black and white.
Its scales blaze in the red-hot sun,
It hisses and it slithers across the ground, the dusty ground.
It is the complete opposite to a lion,
Bold but unhurting.
Dark, like black marble.
It has the colours of a peacock
But the strength of the mighty elephant.
I will look after it like myself and only myself.
I will treat it like the moon.
Slither my animal, slither my animal,
Away to the country.
Away, go away -
Go.

Lewis Winzar (9)
Bedonwell Junior School, Belvedere

Leopard

My leopard is orange like the sun,
He's black and white, like an eclipse
and stars around it.
His magnificent colours stand out for miles
like a lighthouse.
He moves like thunder flashing at light speed.
Half of my leopard is orange and
the other half is white all dressed with
the blackness of Hell.
I will drive away any people who try to eat you,
For you are my only friend.
Listen . . .
I will not let you die,
I cannot bear to live without you, my friend.

Jamie Williams (9)
Bedonwell Junior School, Belvedere

My Precious Tiger

My tiger is orange like the sparkling sun
Orange like a sunset
Orange like fishes in the sea
His roar is like a thousand drums
My tiger is striped, like a rainbow rising
He is like a blazing hot fire
Half of him is dark with blackness and
Half of him is orange like a fish, swimming
His back light, darkness into light
His nose is flashing red
His forehead is striped like a zebra
He resembles the sunset
I will give him some fine water to drink
With you I will drive away my enemies
Let them drink from the well -
The river belongs to me and my tiger
Drink my precious tiger, I am here to guard you!

Sonam Sadhra (10)
Bedonwell Junior School, Belvedere

The Storm

Wind whipped his hissing hair,
Filled up with anger,
As he was whizzing through the air.

Lightning angrily flashed,
Grabbed a car,
Which he bashed and smashed.

Sea crashed against the rocks,
Gulped down a ship
And shook his silvery locks.

Thunder rumbled and turned away,
The storm was over,
But would come back another day.

Molly England (11)
Bedonwell Junior School, Belvedere

My Magnificent Cheetah

My magnificent cheetah is orange
Like an evening sun, setting.
Orange like a tan in the summer morning.
Orange like juice being poured into a glass.

He is fast, like a shooting star,
His shoulders move up and down
While you quiver with fear.
He roars like a volcano ready to erupt.

He is night and day,
The summer and winter,
He is night and day and
He is your air.

I will give my life to save yours,
If poachers come, I shall back them off
With my spear!
Run, run around,
Run, be free;
Run with me.

Lauren O'Brien (9)
Bedonwell Junior School, Belvedere

Party Mayhem

Party, party!
Oh no!
Who should come or who should go?
Auntie Rosie, she's so nosy!
Uncle Joe, he's so slow!
Cousin Billy, he's so silly!
Grandma Nora, you can't ignore her!
Grandpa John, he sleeps for so long!
Best friend Bella, she's such a big teller!
Big brother Dan, he hates to eat ham!
None of these are right for my party!

Alice Young (10)
Bedonwell Junior School, Belvedere

Global Warming

'What's global warming?'
'It's the heating of the Earth.
In fifty years time there could be tornadoes
In Spain and tsunamis in Perth.'

'I still don't get it!'
'Look, when we go in our car,
We send gas into the sky.
It's burning a hole in the atmosphere,
And to icebergs we'll say bye-bye!'

'I get it now, I see what you mean
We'll have to stop going in cars and
I'll have to walk to Dean's.
What terrible things will happen?
We can't have tsunamis in Perth,
millions could be wiped out.'

'My boy, you've got it!
Now preach to your football friends.
Now make sure you build a higher Thames Barrier
And make sure this Earth will never end.'

Sukvinder Sodhi (9)
Bedonwell Junior School, Belvedere

Tiger

Tiger is yellow,
Tiger is black,
Tiger walks along
With stripes on his back.

Tiger runs fast,
Tiger runs quick,
He doesn't even wait
For even a click.

Naomi Lee (7)
Bedonwell Junior School, Belvedere

My PS2

I like to play on my PS2
I don't know why, but I just do.
I think I have twenty games
But I don't know all of their names.
I like playing Burnout, it's my favourite game
Sometimes it's easy but sometimes a pain.
I'm allowed to play on Saturday and Sunday
And if I'm good, I'm allowed to play ten hours a day.
I play with my dad which isn't cool,
He always wins and I always lose.
My brother joins in the fun
When he sees his toys he makes a run.
I'm packing up the PS2,
All the fun is over.
I have to wait until next weekend
For all the fun to start again.

Dominic Chahal (8)
Bedonwell Junior School, Belvedere

Friends For Evermore

We are all very good friends,
We will all stay together to the end.
Friends are our loyal names
Friendship is our noble game,
All of us are going to be together
That is a promise, forever and ever.
All of us staring at the sea,
What a wonder, as we buckle our knees.
A beautiful wonder that we all know
For our friendship will shine and also shall glow.
What a pleasure to put in mind
That your friends will be with you all behind.

Deborah Mary Adebiyi (8)
Bedonwell Junior School, Belvedere

Drowning

The deck creaks and the thunder roars
A terrible groaning fills the corridors
A sound of horrible suffering
Water spatters ever faster
Engulfing life itself
Cannot breathe
I see red
Red billowing from somewhere near
It's still, quiet, peaceful in fact
Suddenly, darkness
Cold, menacing darkness traps me
Visions of selfishness and greed
Creeping ever closer, hatred burning
Then from out of nowhere, light pours through
Extinguishing the hate and misery
A new scene appears
Golden, blooming flowers and trees with ripe and rosy apples
Twinkling streams with violets at their rim
Children playing happily, enjoying themselves
And then something catches my eye
With dreadful fear, I twitch my head
And see right there
A family,
But not just any family
My family, tears in their eyes
Waving goodbye . . .

James Sutton (10)
Bedonwell Junior School, Belvedere

School Is Cool

Monday to Friday we go to school
We learn lots of stuff that is really cool
Literacy, maths, science subjects, so many
But believe it or not, it doesn't cost a penny.

My favourite subject is maths, it's the best
But when the bell goes I'm glad of a rest
We can go out and play with all our friends
It's always sad when the bell goes, it ends.

In the corridors, for safety we walk
When the teacher is speaking, we listen, don't talk
But out of this greatest thing
Is assembly, when we get to sing.

So here it is, I've said it all
Monday to Friday, we have a ball
Just one thing about school to tell
The best thing about it is, Bedonwell!

Shannon Scolding (8)
Bedonwell Junior School, Belvedere

Ruby-Red Roses

Roses are sparkling red, violets are twinkling blue,
Bluebells ringing just like you, so listen to the noises
Of bells around you.
So ruby-red roses are like love,
Shining yellow sunflowers glow like the sun.
Tulips are ruby-red,
The sky is a soft blue and the sun is a blinding light.
Daisies are soft white and so are lilies;
Just like ruby-red roses.
Colourful freesias make the air smell sweet
And yellow daffodils are planted on many streets.
Carnations are colourful, like the rainbow
And all flowers are pretty and make you feel happy.

Molly Patterson (7)
Bedonwell Junior School, Belvedere

I Wish It Would Snow

At night when I lay in my bed
The thing that comes into my head
Is will it snow by morning?
I close my eyes and I start yawning

The next day my wish comes true
I think about what I'm going to do
I run outside in the snow
And build three snowmen in a row

My hands are freezing because of the ice
But playing with snow is very nice
Throwing snowballs is great fun
I hope that we don't get some sun

Dad throws a snowball in my face
Then we have a running race
I fall head first in the snow
Then my dad lays down low

The snow keeps falling through the night
It's still snowing when it gets light
Hooray! that means no school today
Let's go outside and have a play!

Luke Parsons (9)
Bedonwell Junior School, Belvedere

Footballers

Balls, boots and kits and socks.
That's the life of footballers.
Whistling, jeering and shouting managers,
Cheering fans and clapping crowds.

There's no place he'd rather be
Than working around the pitch
Listening to the winners sing
Watching the players go around.

Sam Baker (6)
Bessemer Grange Primary School, London

The Poppy Field

The sky is cloudy
The red poppies are growing,
Swish, swish went the wind.

The wind blows, *swoosh, whoosh,*
The clouds are going *swish swish,*
The sky looks pretty.

The Earth is round,
The sunny red sun glows,
The poppies blow swish.

Then winter blows,
The sky goes grey and dark black,
It makes me happy.

Wish swishes the wind green,
The sky is blue and warm,
Beautiful poppy.

Sydney Sinclair (7)
Bessemer Grange Primary School, London

Footballers

Team, boots and trainers and T-shirts,
That's the life of footballers.
Screaming, shouting and whistling,
Commentators commentating, and squelching mud.

There's no place he'd rather be
Than working on pitches
Listening to the referee's decisions
Watching the ball go around.

Michael Schick (6)
Bessemer Grange Primary School, London

The Waterfall

Boom, blue, blue mountain,
Mountain, spooky with water,
Green grass smashing down.

Sky blue booming down,
Water sliding, *boom*, smashing,
Grass full of wetness.

Water dripping down,
Spooky water smashing down,
Water is dark, *boom*.

River Thames below,
Freezing water bubbles,
White water crashing down.

Shimmery water,
Spooky darkens, *boom*,
Watch the water, *boom*.

Wesley McDonald (7)
Bessemer Grange Primary School, London

Bus Drivers

Steering wheel, key and brakes and seatbelt,
That's the life of bus drivers.
Puff, puff and doors clatter
Doors opening and doors closing.

There's no place he'd rather be
Than working on bus 483
Listening to the sound of the traffic
Watching the bus go up and down.

Joche Adde
Bessemer Grange Primary School, London

Freezing Mountain

The big, tall mountain,
The cold, snowy air makes
The freezing cold sky.

The rock, the green grass,
The white tree is very low,
The snowy mountain.

The blue sky is high,
The blue high sky is freezing,
The big, tall, high sky.

The low grass is cold,
One mountain is freezing,
Grey, white, snowy, black.

Mountain sits still in the ground.

Sam Atkinson (7)
Bessemer Grange Primary School, London

The Field

The sunny green field,
Flowers growing in the sun,
Beautiful flowers.

White snowy mountain,
Fluffy cloud gives me shivers,
Like cotton wool.

The big hills are high,
They are bigger than the sky,
Massive cold mountain.

We are freezing cold,
The sun is shining on me,
Getting in my eyes.

Archie Barker (7)
Bessemer Grange Primary School, London

Season - Haikus

Autumn
The beautiful tree,
Naked and extremely bare,
Her hair swiftly falls.

Spring
The newborn flowers,
Popping up from the brown soil,
Giving such sweet smells.

Summer
The heat is the steam,
From a boiling hot kettle,
No rain for a while!

Winter
The wind, really cold
And as fast as a cheetah,
The snow is coming.

Nabila Ahmed (10)
Bessemer Grange Primary School, London

Cooks

Chopper, fat and pan and eggs,
That's the life of cooks.
Clapping, shouting and whistling
Knives chopping and water running.

There's no place he'd rather be
Than working with delicious foods,
Listening to spoons beating
Watching the mixture go around.

Kyus Holder (6)
Bessemer Grange Primary School, London

Season - Haikus

Spring
When I'm around her,
New life is so close to me,
Is more to be born?

Summer
Hot like a red sun,
In the sky spreading its warmth,
Burning like a fire.

Autumn
The wind is like waves
Whooshing by before you can
Even take a blink.

Winter
She's a bitter frost,
In your eye, white as angels,
Cold like a freezer.

Ruth Auld (11)
Bessemer Grange Primary School, London

Blue Water

Blue, green, mountain sky
The beautiful shiny river
The water-blue sky.

Splash, splash, splish, splosh,
Went the pebbles across the
Water. Small mountain.

The blue sky shining
The mountain is made of rock
The green leafy tree.

The green silver tree
The spooky blue water
The little blue sky.

Wayne O'Brien (7)
Bessemer Grange Primary School, London

Seasonal Haikus

Winter
Snow is trickling down
like tears from a newborn babe
wetting the soft ground.

Spring
A new beginning
for the new year as plants grow
people enjoy spring.

Summer
The sun is like a
ball of hot fire being thrown up
in the atmosphere.

Autumn
All the trees hang their
heads as leaves fall down like rain
autumn - still the same.

John Napoleon Kuofie (11)
Bessemer Grange Primary School, London

The Sunset

The sun is orange,
Summer evening, lovely sky
The sky looks precious.

The sun is lovely, beautiful,
The sunset and the wet trees
The sun is shining.

The sea is lovely, beautiful,
The mountains are orange and big,
It looks like a holiday.

The trees are rustling, breaking.

Sola Kusanu (7)
Bessemer Grange Primary School, London

Seasonal Haikus

Summer
The beautiful red,
hot, bright sun peeps out gladly
from behind the clouds.

Winter
The ice-cold snowmen
build up through the season time
like mounds of ice cream.

Spring
All the little buds
slowly burst their way through like
rain falling from sky.

Autumn
Autumn's crunchy leaves
slowly change colour from green
to soft, muddy brown.

Maryja Cooper (11)
Bessemer Grange Primary School, London

Hot Forest

The bright sun is round,
The forest is dark and black,
There are no clouds there.

There is black, orange,
No people around, no bright moon,
The sunset is bright.

Black forest and
The orange sun is rising,
Evening is glowing.

The bright sun is round,
There is greyish between them,
There are dark colours around.

Kaine Broadhurst (7)
Bessemer Grange Primary School, London

Autumn Trees

Leaves are flowing softly to the floor,
More and more than the year before,
Flittering and swirling around and round,
Then silently touching the cold, soothing ground.

His shadows are like extending arms,
And dangling leaves that look like charms,
His shadows grow as large as they can,
And make delicate bright patterns like a spreading fan.

Lovely colours here, beautiful colours there,
The light wind shakes him and moves his hair,
Green, yellow, red and brown,
He gracefully wears his autumn crown.

Adrienne Good (10)
Bessemer Grange Primary School, London

Hot Mountain

The green tree, country,
The mountain is rock and high,
The sky is orange.

The mountain is high,
The trees are dark and scary,
The sand is crunchy.

I can't see the sun,
It is behind the mountain,
I am very cold.

Amaan Clarke (7)
Bessemer Grange Primary School, London

As Sad As . . .

As sad as a book with no pages,
As sad as animals trapped in cages,
As sad as microphone without a cable,
As sad as a horse without a stable,
As sad as a sun being hidden by clouds,
As sad as a footballer being fowled,
As sad as a handbag that's never been carried,
As sad as a woman that can't get married,
As sad as a beach ball left at sea,
As sad as a baby without a daddy.

Felicia Oduntan (10)
Bessemer Grange Primary School, London

Open Sea

White, white candyfloss,
The water surrounds the mountain,
Clash, clash, bang shudder.

Yellow mountain is hit,
Against the waves free rocky still happy
But, the clouds come out like candyfloss.

Daniel Diguilio (7)
Bessemer Grange Primary School, London

As Happy As . . .

As happy as the sun that's high up in the sky,
As happy as Santa in his sleigh going by,
As happy as flowers standing up tall,
As happy as Cinderella at the prince's ball,
As happy as football when there's someone to kick it,
As happy as a lolly when there's someone to lick it.

Brittney Wallace (11)
Bessemer Grange Primary School, London

As Bored As . . .

I'm as bored as a child without a game,
I'm as bored as a fire without a flame,
I'm as bored as a book that's closed all day,
I'm as bored as a child who cannot play,
I'm as bored as a brain that doesn't have a thought,
I'm as bored as a necklace that never gets bought,
I'm as bored as a player that never gets picked,
I'm as bored as a lolly that doesn't get licked,
I'm as bored as a bully that's got no one to pick on,
I'm as bored as a fraud who's got no one to con,
I'm as bored as player that's got no one to play,
This is the longest and boring day!

James Adcock (11)
Bessemer Grange Primary School, London

Autumn Trees

The beautifully fresh, green, branchy hair,
Sways in the unseen and unheard air,
His hard, brown, string-like, climbable body,
Stays in the same country waiting, waiting, waiting to go,
His feet joined together like a mermaid at sea,
Holding his head up as high as can be,
His hands clapping loudly to an old country tune,
All the sunshine above is losing its pace,
When again will we see his face?

Dilys Akyeampong (10)
Bessemer Grange Primary School, London

The Ocean Island

I see the sparkling, shining water, the shimmering, glistening sand,
The beautiful, shining sun setting in the sky.

I hear the waves calmly flowing over the limpet-covered rocks
And the cracking of the hatching baby turtles, emerging from
The sand, suddenly I hear a whale, wailing out at sea.

I smell the salty air and the lobster fried in lemon.

I taste the traditional food eaten there!
I taste the sparkling, fizzy cocktails,
I taste the cold, sweet ice cream which sends a cold
feeling to my head.

I feel like there is magic in the air and a warm wind across my face,
I feel the particles of sand between my toes.
I feel the warm, foamy water washing it away.

Jennifer Lucy Munden (10)
Collingwood School, Wallington

The Football Match

I see the big players on the half running with the circle ball,
I smell the big, meaty hot dogs and disgusting smell of
cigarettes so pungent!
I taste the hot, steamy taste of hot dogs on my tingling tongue
all through the match,
I hear the crowd cheer as soon as Robben gets the ball
and dribbles it down the line,
I feel the cold breeze on my face as I am sitting on my seat
anxiously waiting for them to score.

Alex Denning (10)
Collingwood School, Wallington

Disaster

I see the disaster, the catastrophe,
the waves which came from the deep, blue sea,
this tsunami has really touched me.

I hear things on the news
about what happened, on Boxing Day last year,
the newsflash just caught my ear.

I smell the danger in the air,
the worst thing that could happen, there,
the bodies, lying still and dead,
the hospital is straight ahead.

I taste the bitterness, it is here,
for all the people that are ill,
I wish there was a special pill,
to make them better, not make them ill.

I feel sad about the disaster occurring,
there is still a great yearning
to help the people whom for so many are caring.

Rosie Maureen Molly Bain (11)
Collingwood School, Wallington

The Great Outdoors!

I see the sparkly, twinkling snowflakes flutter by,
I hear joyful children, laughing and singing merrily,
I smell my brother's hot, fresh fruit muffin smelling very delicious,
I taste wet snowflakes on my tongue,
I feel so freezing that I can't feel my titchy, toes.

Oyinda Ayonrinde (10)
Collingwood School, Wallington

The Nile

I see the glistening sights of Egypt,
All the animals, crocodiles and fishes,
In the depth of wonder, flowing through deserts,
The lovely sparkling Nile.

I smell the beautiful salty waters,
Flowing for miles on end,
Yet flowing, vast through deserts,
It still never ends.

I taste the lovely salty waters,
Whether savoury, sweet, I don't mind,
For I could live on this day by day,
The lovely sparkling Nile.

I hear the gorgeous river splash,
Gently in the breeze,
Yet it does not affect the fishes,
Swimming in freeze.

I feel the lovely touch of the river and wonder,
How people cannot see,
The beauty of the long running Nile,
And wonder how it can be?

Krishan Sareen (9)
Collingwood School, Wallington

The Beach

I see the seagulls gliding swiftly above me,
I hear their mournful cries,
I smell the calm, salty water,
I taste the salt spray from the waves,
I feel the soft, golden sand beneath my feet.

Ashok Menon (10)
Collingwood School, Wallington

The Poetry Competition

I see the children working hard around me,
Sweat mounting on their faces.

I hear the scratching of their pencils,
As they work away.

I smell the air around me, the warmth and familiar
Fragrance of the classroom as I breathe in slowly.

I taste the cold, fresh water and I can feel it running
                                        down my throat.

I can feel the tension around myself, coming from
                                        the other children.

Our entries for the poetry competition have to be in by tomorrow!

Charlotte Brocklesby (10)
Collingwood School, Wallington

Football

I see the perfectly laid pitch with grass as flat as a carpet,
I hear the gigantic roar of the crowd making me tremble,
I smell the fat hot dogs being cooked with the smell
                                        floating around the stadium,
I taste the drink so sweet and the hot dog so spicy,
                                        hot and delicious,
I feel the wonderful heat circling around the stadium.

Daniel Bunting (11)
Collingwood School, Wallington

Winter

I see cold white crisp snow laying on the ground,
I hear people's feet crunching on the snow and
                              children's laughter,
I smell the smoke from people's chimneys as they
       sit by the cosy fire in the warmth of their houses.
I taste lovely warm hot chocolate leaving me with a warm sensation,
I feel as wonderful as the sparkling snowflakes as they descend
                                          on me.

Emma Kenton (11)
Collingwood School, Wallington

My Birthday

I see lots of beautifully wrapped presents on the
                              living room floor,
I hear my friends singing 'Happy Birthday' and
                       shouting 'Hip, hip, hooray!'
I smell the burning of candles on my birthday cake,
I taste my sweets that I got for my birthday,
I feel happy because it's my birthday, hip, hip hooray!

Luke Hannigan (11)
Collingwood School, Wallington

Winter

I see white fluffy cloudy snowflakes falling from the blue carpet sky,
I hear children shouting and crunching on the soft snow,
I smell Christmas dinner coming out from the burning hot oven,
I taste freezing cold snow falling on my tongue,
I feel the cold wintry breeze chilling my face.

Shilpa Suresh (10)
Collingwood School, Wallington

Lucy The Dog

I see Lucy chewing on my nan's best wool,
I smell Christopher's dinner getting cold,
I taste my dinner of mouth-watering chicken fillets,
I hear Christopher shouting at the dog,
I feel wool being wound around my leg by the dog,
I fall over entangled in a mass of wool.

Jordan McGuinness (10)
Collingwood School, Wallington

Winter

I see the cold, harsh winter take the leaves from trees away,
I hear the wind howling, shrieking and screeching,
I smell the Christmas food cooking in the kitchen,
I taste the hot chocolate trickling down my throat,
I feel the cold going through my limbs and I know it's wintertime.

Alexandra Elizabeth Reed (11)
Collingwood School, Wallington

Cricket

I see the ball flying out of bounds,
I hear the quiet buzz of the crowd,
I taste the cooling drink after every over,
I smell the sweet-smelling grass,
I feel the grip in my hand from the bat.

Andrew Searle (11)
Collingwood School, Wallington

Beauty

I have seen the sun, the moon, the stars,
Sparkling in the day, the night like it's ours,
I hear the lovely ocean roar,
I'm sorry for the people who haven't heard that before,
I smell the smell of fragrant pine,
It smells go good, it smells so fine,
I taste the taste of chocolate milkshake,
Not being able to resist is a big mistake,
I feel all of these in my mind,
People think this beauty is hard to find.

Jack Aguéra (10)
Collingwood School, Wallington

The Go-Kart Tournament

I see go-karts racing on the racetrack,
I smell the petrol of the go-karts,
I taste the burgers sizzling on the BBQ,
I hear the go-karts racing along,
I feel the breeze of the go-karts against my face.

Matthew Brewer (10)
Collingwood School, Wallington

The Rugby Match

I see the rugby ball in the air,
I smell the sweaty rugby players,
I taste the fat lip I got playing rugby,
I hear the roar from the crowd as a try is scored,
I feel the ball hitting me in the face.

Harry Jones (9)
Collingwood School, Wallington

Rose

I smell the sweet, smothering scent of the rose's centre,
I taste the cool dew drop from the rose's flower,
I hear the breeze flutter the rose petals around calmly,
I see the dark red flower floating above me in the air,
I feel the soft sleepy touch of the rose's petals surrounding me.
I'm in darkness!

Fern Colepio (9)
Collingwood School, Wallington

The Rainforest

I can see the great trees as tall as they are,
I can hear the waterfalls pounding so fast,
I smell the tropical flowers' wonderful fragrance,
I taste the wet air on my lips,
I feel the power of this place.

Darren Mindham (10)
Collingwood School, Wallington

Pubs

I see people shouting in the pubs,
I hear the sound of drunk waiters laughing,
I smell the whiff of cigarettes in the air,
I taste the bitterness of beer and ale on my tongue,
I feel idiotic drinking so much beer.

Tobi Adedayo Adeyemi (10)
Collingwood School, Wallington

All Around

I see myself designing a new type of bridge because
I want to be an engineer,
I hear nothing because I wish the world was silent,
I smell fresh air because I am in the countryside,
I taste toothpaste in my mouth,
I feel my heart pounding quickly.

James William Acquaye Nortey-Glover (10)
Collingwood School, Wallington

Winter

I see the white carpet of snow,
I smell the sizzling bacon in the pan,
I taste the cold snowflakes melting on my warm tongue,
I hear many children playing in the freezing snow,
I feel the cold wind impact on my face.

William Parsons (9)
Collingwood School, Wallington

The Sea

I see the bright blue sea,
I smell the salty, deep, blue sea,
I taste the cold vanilla ice cream on my tongue,
I hear the splashing on the sea,
I feel the sand running between my toes.

Heather Filby (9)
Collingwood School, Wallington

My Football Match

I see the churned up mud all across the field,
I smell the beautiful smell of hot chocolate in the morning,
I taste the wet sweat in my dried up mouth,
I hear the sound of children screaming for both battling teams,
I feel the hard leather ball whacking across my face.
That is what I call a football match.

Alfie Barnard Ford (9)
Collingwood School, Wallington

Tilly

I see her dive through the bouncy waves,
I smell her fish as she eats it,
I taste the salty water in the sea,
I hear her squeak as she talks to me,
I feel her rubbery skin against my arm.

Eleanor Blackford (9)
Collingwood School, Wallington

The Chelsea Victory

I see Eider Gudjohnsen in the distance,
I smell the victory for Chelsea,
I taste the pressure building up,
I hear the chanting of the crowd,
I feel elated when I score a goal.

Jordan Pini (9)
Collingwood School, Wallington

The Dragon

I see its scaly skin, vibrating as it swoops down towards me,
I smell the smoke, it breathes, as it scorches my blistering back,
I taste the air, it tastes of bitter death,
I hear laughter from the past as this is surely the end,
I feel flames licking my back as it slowly plays with me, its prey!

Will Evans (9)
Collingwood School, Wallington

On The Banks Of The Nile

The Nile flood
Turns fields to mud,
The desert sand
To lush green land,
People suffering every day,
The Nile is like a life saving ray,
The current has such great force
It is the Egyptian life source.

Alex Gillies (10)
Compton & Up Marden CE Primary School, Chichester

Under The Ground I Found

Golden mirrors painted with colours,
Hieroglyphs and pictures that mean nothing to me.

Ancient amulets gleaming gold,
Superior scarabs pictured on walls,
Perfect pendants, Cleopatra's maybe,
Huge headdresses with flawless patterns.

Amazing ankhs, a sign of life,
Symbolising power, worn only by the pharaohs of then.

Izzy Weston-Goodman (11)
Compton & Up Marden CE Primary School, Chichester

Egyptian War

Armies fighting like a ferocious bear,
As they're firing in the air,
Fierce as they come,
They ride into battle,
Falcons fly overhead, like a load of hungry vultures.

Men are dying, men are living,
As their wives and children cry,
While they make the tombs,
Fire in their eyes, like a dragon's lava
Pouring out of its mouth,
This is the biggest battle of their lives,
Chariots tip, carry on fighting on foot.

They go home,
To see their family.
It is over.

Connor Cunningham (11)
Compton & Up Marden CE Primary School, Chichester

All That Glitters, Egyptian Treasure

All that glitters, all that's gold,
Egyptian treasures both old and gold.
Necklaces, bracelets, worn by who?
By pharaohs, Cleopatra, could it be true?

All that glitters, all that glimmers,
Pretty pendants, golden mirrors.
Beautiful brooches, buried in pyramids.
Excellent emeralds scattered around,
Some have been lost, some have been found.

Ellie Hoar (10)
Compton & Up Marden CE Primary School, Chichester

The Nile

A man went to war for his wife,
He slashed people with his huge knife,
He was as strong as a pyramid,
He came back to his house and hid,
He went to his soft squishy bed,
To rest his heavy sweating head.

When he finally woke up,
He drank from a beautiful cup,
He got up and scratched his itchy head,
And jumped off his smelly old bed,
And saw what he thought was a sparrow,
But it was a deadly arrow,
It hit him with deadly sharp aim,
A Libyan was to blame.

His wife was very despaired,
As she stood there and stared and stared,
His unhappy wife cried and cried,
When the soldier got mummified,
She wasn't exactly filled with glee,
But that's how the Nile came to be.

Jack Coles (10) & Nathan Etherington (11)
Compton & Up Marden CE Primary School, Chichester

Buried Treasure

A gold earring as shiny as the sun,
A lucky girdle as pretty as the sky,
A silver ring that shimmers like the moon,
A turquoise, an amethyst and a bronze mirror too!

A special ankh - a symbol of life,
A magic amulet - to save its wearer from evil,
Lucky carvings on a royal bracelet,
Green feldspar, a statue and a collar of gold!

Charlotte Mills (9)
Compton & Up Marden CE Primary School, Chichester

Kill For The Jewels

Jewels awaiting in the pyramids as the pharaoh walks outside,
Can the thief resist the temptation to kill him for the prize?
He knew the kill would start a war
So he trained his army more and more.
So he slayed the pharaoh from head to toe,
Then snatched the jewels, planned as so.
The evidence started a war in the sand
Out far in the desert land.
As thousands of feet thudded with a pound
War men's bodies fall to the ground.
Armies fighting like a ferocious bear
Firing arrows up in the air.
Fierce as they come, they ride into battle,
And as they come they ride into hassle.
Committing suicide, the thief chops off his own head
War is over, the great thief's dead.

Liam Dixon (10)
Compton & Up Marden CE Primary School, Chichester

The Great Pyramids

P yramids have thousands of bricks,
Wh Y ? to make them really tall.
R ed land is full of pyramids,
A nubis embalms the dead pharaohs.
M ummies run around after their children.
I f you put a mummy in a sarcophagus,
   you'll have to put it in a pyramid.
D oors of granite and rock.

Charlotte Hill (9)
Compton & Up Marden CE Primary School, Chichester

The Pyramid

It towers above the desert sands,
Guarded by the sphinx.
Pharaohs buried deep inside
In sarcophaguses as tall as the temple of Re,
Traps for careless tomb robbers
From the further parts of Egypt.

Jewels and gems glistening like the morning sun,
Blue and gold death mask on the mummy like a beautiful statue,
The Eye of Horus bringing luck to the burial tombs.

Thoth weighing the hearts of mummified pharaohs
Seeing if they'll have glory, or death.
In the Netherlands, or with the Devourer.

Anubis embalming and carrying the lost,
Forgotten souls of pharaohs to Osiris in Duat,
Never to be seen in the light of day again.

Luke Isom (9)
Compton & Up Marden CE Primary School, Chichester

Anubis

The lord of the sacred land
With a jackal's head.
Is as solemn as a water lily just blooming,
When steering the boat into the afterlife.

Many bodies pass through his hands,
all wrapped in snow-white cloth,
No brain they have nor organs,
For they are trapped in canopied jars.

The son of the god of the sun,
Whom sails across the skies,
In his solar boat (the sun)
The creator of the great Egyptian world.

Thomas Woodcock (11) & Jack Mannings (9)
Compton & Up Marden CE Primary School, Chichester

The Battle Of Egyptian Love

'The Hittites have declared war with us,' the Pharaoh cried,
Those words he spoke were like daggers down my throat.

'My love you are my Isis,'
'And you are my Osiris,'
'I have a duty to go to war for you,'
'You are my saviour true and true.'

'My return is in the hands of Anubis now,
So just relax and hope me good luck, but don't ask me how.'

When I stood upon the battlefield,
Real hope and belief ran through my skin,
As I knew that I would fight and win,
The clashing of swords and the rattling of shields.

The duet was like thunder and lightning,
The sounds were very, very frightening,

I suddenly began to fear, that we'd never be able to
                                          have a cheer,
But my determination to keep my life, was as strong
                                          as my love for my wife
The force of Seth flew by,
It finally looked like we weren't going to die.

The Hittites were suffering in pain on the ground,
My mates laughed and looked around.

'You are my pharaoh riding in the chariot of my love,'
'Welcome home brave soldier.'

Charles Wade-Palmer (9)
Compton & Up Marden CE Primary School, Chichester

The Colossal Siege

The battle had started,
The bloodshed had begun,
Arrows were whistling,
Skewering the glare of the sun.
Blood was oozing,
Out of the mortal remains,
Armour was glinting,
On the desert plains.

On top of tombs,
Pyramids were tumbling,
Whilst the mighty sphinx,
Began crumbling,
Infantries vision becomes darkness,
Vultures circling the skies,
Plucking the flesh off the soldiers bodies,
As their lifeless ghost cries.

Anubis had a task to do,
Embalming all the dead,
The armies glanced at the corpses,
Spun round and fled,
All was won,
But all was lost,
The death of one thousand lives,
Was the Egyptians' biggest cost.

Rory Watson (11) & Hugh Sawers (10)
Compton & Up Marden CE Primary School, Chichester

Isis

Isis,
Goddess of nature,
And the great enchantress,
Her hair flowed like a black river,
And on her head, the throne of Egypt,
Which is the hieroglyph, of her name.

Charlotte Beaman (10)
Compton & Up Marden CE Primary School, Chichester

Georgia

This is my best friend,
Our friendship will never end.

She is called Georgia Loud,
Trust me, she's popular, always near a crowd.

She likes horses just like me,
I like dogs, so does she.

She always tells jokes and makes me giggle,
When we go to a disco we dance till we wiggle.

Her smile brightens up the day,
Nothing is OK when she is away.

We are best mates and that's a fact,
Forever and ever we made a pact.

Abbie Fletcher (10)
Crofton Anne Dale Junior School, Fareham

My Grandad

My grandad is sweet-hearted,
Kind and gentle,
He loves me lots,
He's a great man,
He thinks I'm smart,
He makes my ideas come true,
He grants my wishes,
He takes me to football matches,
He takes me to the beach,
That's my wonderful
Smart, wicked grandad!

Karly Higgs (9)
Crofton Anne Dale Junior School, Fareham

Tsunami Poem

People playing near the sea,
Beautiful beach,
Holiday fun,
Then the wave came crashing in,
Panic,
People running, people pushing,
News reports thousands dead,
World shocked,
Homes destroyed,
Lonely children crying everywhere,
People praying to God,
How could this happen?

Hannah Miller (7)
Crofton Anne Dale Junior School, Fareham

Polka Dots

They come in pink,
They come in blue,
They come in green,
And purple too.
You can find them on shorts and shirts,
Babies' tops and ladies' skirts,
They come on walls and even balls,
On circus fools and paddling pools,
Polka dots pop up in every place,
Even on your pretty face.

Beth Sadler (9)
Crofton Anne Dale Junior School, Fareham

The Sea

The salty odour hits you as you stroll along the beach,
The seagulls plunging into the sea with an irritated screech,
The rolling waves gently breaking upon the velvety sand,
The sea is as unpredictable as a game of chess, and,
I'm in the boat skimming the surface, the rider of the waves,
The island's in the distance, with their long-forgotten caves.

The wind is rising, tying knots into my hair,
The sea is a powerful weapon, proceed with much care,
The wind howling through the sails,
The sheets of rain forming a translucent, charming veil,
Intense irregular movements throw about our battered boat,
We are desperately trying to keep this ship afloat.

Home again, home sweet home,
Safe again, hot soup alone
Has revived my senses,
I ride the waves to my own expenses.

Sophie Coleman (11)
Crofton Anne Dale Junior School, Fareham

Hamsters

H amsters are really small,
A nd you might not notice them at all,
M y little hamster sleeps all day,
S o she wakes at night to play,
T o my surprise, she escapes again,
E ven when it's suppertime, then,
R uns away to hide from me,
S o I tempt her back with some tea.

William Downham (9)
Crofton Anne Dale Junior School, Fareham

Night

Night is like a thief
Stealing away the sunlight.

Night is like a silent deadly killer
Who takes your life away.

Night is like a discourteous crude joker
Waking you up like a devastating nightmare.

Night is like a virus
Destroying everything in its path.

Night could have a scarred face,
But maybe none at all.

Night is like a maze
No exit, none at all.

Night is like an electric fence,
Night is as secretive as Area 51
Night is a flytrap waiting for its prey
Night's a labyrinth
A killer bat is night taking away the light.

Daniel Fisher (11)
Crofton Anne Dale Junior School, Fareham

After The Tsunami

After the tsunami on Boxing Day,
Daddy said 'Farewell,'
We watched him go,
As he smiled and winked his eye,
'Be good,' he called with a very big sigh,
'Look after your mother and brother,
I don't know what I'm doing,
I can't really say,
My help is needed to bring water and food,
I'm taking it to the people and children,
Who need our care and help.'
'Good luck Daddy and we will see you soon!'

Laura Kingston (8)
Crofton Anne Dale Junior School, Fareham

The Sea

Splashing and sploshing,
Through the whole of the day,
Where dolphins are playing,
Far, far away.

The sea is alive,
With quick-moving tails,
Splish, splash, splish, splash,
There go the whales!

But dorsal fins now begin to appear
The whole of the ocean trembles with fear,
Sharks are swimming around and around,
Ripping through the water without a sound.

The water begins to redden with blood,
Bodies and bones fall quick with a thud,
The sharks have now finished their meal,
But the dolphins' wounds will just not heal.

Jessica Edney (8)
Crofton Anne Dale Junior School, Fareham

Volcano

Volcano,
An evil force powerful enough to destroy whole countries,
Trying to escape.
A bubbling cauldron of fear and pain heading towards civilisation,
A brightly coloured flower, beautiful yet deadly,
A great mound of anger let loose,
Beware,
Volcano, destroyer of lives,
Beware.

Isabelle Coleman (11)
Crofton Anne Dale Junior School, Fareham

The Beach

I lay on the beach
With sand in my toes
Is anyone here? Nobody knows,
I get up and go and swim in the sea,
I see children swimming quite close to me,
I laugh with joy and join in the fun,
But while I'm not looking the dark has begun,
The moon shining bright up in the sky,
And then all the children wave goodbye!
I go home and have a shower,
I think of the children hour by hour,
I get into bed and sleep with a flower,
As morning begins it's just God's power,
I have my breakfast, cool as cool,
To help me swim in the pool!

Jasmine Kershaw (10)
Crofton Anne Dale Junior School, Fareham

My Mum

She's a big cuddly toy,
A quiet sleeping cat,
A diary of thoughts,
A soft, gentle cloud,
A rabbit bouncing around the house,
A dog asleep on a mat,
But sometimes she's a tell-you-off teddy bear,
A lion chasing mouse,
A volcano about to erupt,
But best of all she's my mum.

Hannah Dewane (10)
Crofton Anne Dale Junior School, Fareham

Waddling Penguins

Penguins waddle to and fro,
Eating chocolate as they go,
Their socks are stripy just like mine,
And I have seen them drinking wine,
They live in water icy cold,
Swimming happily young and old,
When moonlight comes the children yawn,
Then wait till tomorrow when they can explore!
When dawn is near the children wake,
And give their penguin parents a shake,
They all live happily, never fear,
Because their waddling parents are near!

Brooklyn Barber (10)
Crofton Anne Dale Junior School, Fareham

Flowers

Flowers in the morning,
That brighten up the day,
You have to love the flowers,
In all kinds of ways.
Tulips and daisies and roses too,
There are lots of flowers in the world,
You don't have to choose.
Bluebells and lilies,
All nicely set in a row,
When I skip past them,
I smell them as I go.

Kayleigh Fowler (10)
Crofton Anne Dale Junior School, Fareham

Make A Wish

If wishes came true,
Every wish you made,
I hope you wouldn't wish,
For a bucket and spade.

I hope you would think,
About all the others,
The mums and the dads,
The sisters and brothers.

And what about people,
Who have no home?
Or poor young orphans
Left all alone?

So when it comes round to your birthday wish,
The best thing you could do,
Is think of other people,
And believe that wishes come true.

Madeleine Horst (10)
Crofton Anne Dale Junior School, Fareham

Tabby

Tabby race,
Tabby run,
Tabby really having fun,
Tabby slow,
Tabby stop,
Tabby just then drops right off,
Tabby wakes,
Tabby aims,
Tabby falls asleep again,
And that's Tabby's life!

Josie Bagley (8)
Crofton Anne Dale Junior School, Fareham

The Alien

He was small and green,
Landing in his flying machine,
With short, stubby legs,
And a head full of pegs.
'Why have you come here?'
Says a boy with fear.
The alien replies,
'From far in the skies,
I have travelled young sir,
To see such splendour and
Marvellous things occur,
But here I see the heart of gold,
The face of joy
And all this I see in you, dear boy!'

Jordan Pearson (9)
Crofton Anne Dale Junior School, Fareham

Springtime

S un grows the roses,
P ots full of primroses,
R ed-hot on cold noses,
I n the winter the ice was cold,
N ow the days have a sun of gold,
G rassy fields have badgers bold,
T eensy bits of grass are swaying,
I know just why,
M y heart is saying:
E very good day is spring!

Laura Macfarlane (9)
Crofton Anne Dale Junior School, Fareham

Dancing

Can't wait for Tuesday night,
It's dance club at the hall,
Upon the stage and in the lights,
The glitterball is shining bright,
We're taught to dance,
To new romance,
We love to move,
To disco groove,
An hour has past,
It's gone too fast,
Another dance is what we seek,
Alas we have to wait for next week.

Kelly-Marie Holmes (8)
Crofton Anne Dale Junior School, Fareham

Shark Alert

Scaly shark,
Pointy nose shark,
Man-eating shark,
Call shark anything on land,
But not in water,
In case he snaps
You *up!*

Alexandra McRobbie (8)
Crofton Anne Dale Junior School, Fareham

I Want A . . .

I want a toy from my mummy,
I want a cake for my tummy,
I want a book from my gran,
I want a spoon and a pan,
I want a picture from my aunt,
I want a flowery plant,
I want a pen from my dad,
I want a monkey that's mad,
I want a piggy bank . . .
And some money from Frank,
I want a mirror from Bell and Bob,
I want a wooden doorknob,
I want a horse that says, 'Neigh,'
And a saddle from May,
I want a pencil from my brother Mike,
I want a big, red shiny bike,
Last but not least I want a pet.

But Mum says, 'I want doesn't get!'

Poppy Saville (10)
Crofton Anne Dale Junior School, Fareham

Victoria

V ictoria is my sister,
I know when she's about,
C lutter is her second name,
T idy she is not
O pen to talk to, always there for fun,
R un to for cuddles,
I couldn't wish for a better sister,
A better sister? There is none!

Sam Goodsell (7)
Crofton Anne Dale Junior School, Fareham

Who Wants To Be A Cat?

Who wants to be a cat, lying on a mat?
Eating all day until it is fat,
Chasing mice if the weather is nice,
Or purring by the fire if the weather is dire,
Sitting in a tree,
Looking down at you and me,
Thinking how clever I am,
Don't you wish you were me,
Who wants to be a cat?

I do!

Audrey Macleod (10)
Crofton Anne Dale Junior School, Fareham

My Best Friend!

My best friend has long wavy hair,
Her eyes are warm and welcoming,
She makes me laugh when I am down,
And has a smile on my face,
She has a face that has been carved by angels,
She is a dolphin jumping and splashing in the water,
She is bubbly and playful and kind,
She is popcorn popping,
She is my friend!

Madeline Smith (10)
Crofton Anne Dale Junior School, Fareham

The Wedding

Miss Hyde was the bride,
Mr Bloom was the bridegroom,
Miss Staid was the bridesmaid,
Miss Pearl was the flower girl,
Master Doy was the page boy.

Mr Slicker the vicar ran in with a shout,
And said to the congregation, sat all about,
'Quick the bride's mother is stuck in the door,
We'll be here till Christmas that much is sure!'
So they all pulled and pulled but no luck,
She really was completely stuck.

'It was a very funny sight,'
The photographer declared,
'My wedding photo scenery
Is usually the sun,
Not the bride's mother's bum!'

Sophie Charlotte Mary Keen (8)
Crofton Anne Dale Junior School, Fareham

Funky Friends Poem

F unky friends are really cool,
R ebecca is my funky friend,
I ntelligent she is,
E veryone likes her,
N o one hates her,
D o you like her?
S ay 'Yes!'

Gemma Arnfield (9)
Crofton Anne Dale Junior School, Fareham

Toby The Dog

He is a box of Toblerones,
He is soft as a fluffy polar bear,
He is sunny as the beach,
As energetic as a mad professor,
As black as the midnight sky,
I like Toby just the way he is.

Alice Tucker (9)
Crofton Anne Dale Junior School, Fareham

My Best Friend

My best friend is Maddy Smith,
She likes reading lots of myths,
Our friendship is everlasting,
I will never let her start fasting,
Because she is lovely as she is!

Laura Green (11)
Crofton Anne Dale Junior School, Fareham

My Friend Erin

As soft as a cushion,
As kind as a dolphin,
As fast as a car,
As brainy as a scientist,
Always there for me.

Jenna Andrews (9)
Crofton Anne Dale Junior School, Fareham

The New Disease

There is a new horrible disease,
It's not a cough or a sneeze,
It's about you being late,
You book for seven arrive at eight.

My mum's got it very bad,
And she caught it off my dad,
My mum and dad are always late,
Forever making people wait.

The sad thing is they are always slow,
But that's the way it has to go,
This is a warning to take on board,
It really must not be ignored!

Put up posters in your street,
Tell all the people that you meet,
Before you catch it, warn your friends,
Until they get ill and meet their ends!

Emma Manning (10)
Egerton CE Primary School, Ashford

Crow Surprise

There was a young girl from Ho,
Who had a noisy black crow,
Then her crow flew away,
And came back the next day,
With three chicks and a girlfriend named Flo!

Gabriella Hasham (9)
Egerton CE Primary School, Ashford

My Kennings Of Me

Housework hater
Horse lover
Fussy eater
Brother shover.

Great helper
Avid reader
Nature adventurer
Good deeder.

Patient waiter
Cruelty hater
Cross with my brother
Like him there's no other!

Holly Smith (10)
Egerton CE Primary School, Ashford

My Dad

Cow-milker
Tea-drinker
Pheasant-shooter
Dog-lover
Bad-dresser
Cat-hater
Fantastic-drawer
Loud-snorer
Good-swimmer
Tractor-driver
Food-eater
But altogether,
The best father.

Katie Hope (10)
Egerton CE Primary School, Ashford

The Flying Creatures!

Fluttering around everywhere they go,
Soft wings glittering with colours unique,
Buzzing around they're not very slow,
Delicate creatures just like antiques,
The world in their hands of which humans trust,
Careful, not harmful and trustworthy too,
Work hard all day to help others, they must,
To help all adults and children like you,
Light, which they produce, of which we all use,
Helping is what they do for everyone,
They like light colours, the colours that fuse,
Flying fast through clouds, until they are gone,
Twinkling through the night lights of the world,
Fairies do all of this and rule the world!

Amy Heuch (10)
Egerton CE Primary School, Ashford

Me

Smart-dresser
Fussy-eater
Vegetable-hater
Animal-liker
Bike-rider
Cricket-player
Football-lover
Goal-keeper
Good-kicker
Man Utd-supporter
Poem-writer
That is me!

Ricky Ralph (10)
Egerton CE Primary School, Ashford

Alone In My Room

Alone in my room
In my own little world
I lie on my bed
All snuggled up and curled.

Around my black cat
Whose soft rhythmical purr
Lulls me to sleep
With her velvety fur.

I think about things
That have happened that day
And plan what to do
When I go out and play.

I play with the toys
That are kept on my bed
The best one of all
Is my mummy's old ted.

My cat breaks the spell
As she jumps on the floor
And I rejoin the world
As I walk through the door.

Beatrice Calver (10)
Egerton CE Primary School, Ashford

Fish

Weed eater
Sea swimmer
Rock hider
Current rider
Egg layer
Shark dinner!

Alex Blowers (9)
Egerton CE Primary School, Ashford

Kennings

Ball-chaser
Hole-digger
Stick-fetcher
Food-gobbler.

Fast-runner
Sound-sleeper
Face-licker
Loud-snorer.

Deep-barker
Sweet-dreamer
Fur-groomer
Heel-nipper

Have you guessed yet?

Rebecca Amos (11)
Egerton CE Primary School, Ashford

Kennings About Myself

Girl hater
Food eater
Mayhem maker
House shaker
Football lover
Brother shover
Chocolate guzzler
Friend puzzler
Pencil blunter
Comic collector
Rude speaker
Attention seeker
TV watcher
Now I gotcha!

Josh Deane (10)
Egerton CE Primary School, Ashford

Sweet Menu

Raspberry mousse and chocolate cake,
Great to eat and easy to make.

Strawberry shortcake and iced bun,
Eating these treats is really good fun.

Angel cookies and vanilla ice cream,
Sweets that are tasty, and shall make you beam.

Jammy biscuit and gummy bears,
Better than apricots, carrots or pears.

Pick 'n' mix sweets and apple pie,
The more sweets you like, the more sweets you'll buy.

Or then there is broccoli and cabbage to eat,
But the foods above are a child's real treat.

Rachel Green (11)
Egerton CE Primary School, Ashford

I Am?

Chip-seller
Calorie-maker
Toy-giver
Milk-shaker
Meal-tempter
Buyer-hunter
Burger-sizzler
Money-cruncher . . .

McDonald's!

Aaron Parr (10)
Egerton CE Primary School, Ashford

There Was A Young Girl

There was a young girl
Who went to the pool
Did ten laps
And then went to school.

She got to school late
The teacher was mad
She went to her desk
And got out her pad.

She went home
And read a cookery book
Made a pizza
She was a very good cook.

Her dad ate the pizza
Said it was good
She went out
And bought him a pud.

She felt hungry
So she made him some rice
Then some cake
It was nice.

It was her birthday
She was ten
She got lots of presents
Including a pen.

They went to an Indian
For a treat
Their waiter was funny
His name was Pete.

Her birthday was over
They went back home
She missed her mum
She was in Rome.

Ruby Gretton (10)
Egerton CE Primary School, Ashford

A Shakespeare Parody

Double, double,
In deep trouble,
Numbers twist,
And spellings muddle.

My teacher comes along this way,
Looking at me in dismay,
I turn around and just ignore,
The look that's on her face once more.

Double, double,
In deep trouble,
Numbers twist,
And spellings muddle.

The head comes and inspects my book,
He gives me a most filthy look,
I say to him that I'll do better,
Next week when I write my letter.

Double, double,
Out of trouble,
Head's impressed,
And things aren't muddled!

Sophie Major (11)
Egerton CE Primary School, Ashford

The Boy From Smarden

There was a boy from Smarden
Who drove all the way to London
His car broke down
In the middle of town
He burped and said, 'I do beg your pardon!'

Seth Matthews (11)
Egerton CE Primary School, Ashford

Guess What I Am?

Rat-snatcher
Mouse-catcher
Hard-scratcher
Strong-biter
Little-purrer
Fire-hogger
Big-eater
Good-sleeper

Can you guess?
It's a cat.

Jennie Mackay (10)
Egerton CE Primary School, Ashford

My Kennings

Weird squeaker
Little creeper

Great eater
Drinks a litre

Dog hater
No traitor

Fluffy snuggler
Attacks wuggler.

Bryony Davison (10)
Egerton CE Primary School, Ashford

Misery

Misery is grey, like a thunderstorm floating over me,
Misery sounds like lightning striking a tree,
Misery smells like smoke,
Misery looks like rain pouring down,
Misery tastes like sick at the back of my throat.

Sophie Gardiner (9)
Four Elms Primary School, Edenbridge

Hate

Hate is red, like an explosion.
Hate sounds like someone shouting in your ear.
Hate smells like smoke.
Hate looks like something bubbling.
Hate tastes like bitter lemon.

Christopher Allen (10)
Four Elms Primary School, Edenbridge

Fear

Fear is orange, like fire burning inside me,
Fear sounds like ghosts howling at me,
Fear smells like a rotting fish,
Fear looks like flames growing bigger every minute,
Fear tastes like a mouldy apple.

Abigail Hamblin (9)
Four Elms Primary School, Edenbridge

Love

Love is pink, like my heart floating to a different person,
Love sounds like happiness in the air,
Love smells like perfume on my hand,
Love looks like a cake shaped as a heart,
Love tastes like chocolate cake!

Annie Greenaway (10)
Four Elms Primary School, Edenbridge

Envy

Envy is green, like a shark ready to attack,
It sounds like a steam train roaring through your body,
It smells like the skin of a lemon,
It looks like a lion attacking its prey,
It tastes like a bitter lemon.

Madeleine Knapman (10)
Four Elms Primary School, Edenbridge

Laughter

Laughter is green, like a big glowing star
Laughter sounds like a waterfall of happiness
Laughter smells like the scent of lavender
Laughter looks like a big, cheesy grin
Laughter tastes like melted chocolate.

Kirsty McGregor (9)
Four Elms Primary School, Edenbridge

Hate

Hate is black, like a deadly cave inside.
Hate looks like black darkness.
Hate sounds like crashing waves.
Hate smells like deadly gas.
Hate tastes like an out of date, sour apple.

Ryan Johnson (10)
Four Elms Primary School, Edenbridge

Love

Love is red, like a ladybird,
Love sounds like romantic music,
Love smells like melting chocolate,
Love looks like hearts floating in the beautiful sky,
Love tastes like a chocolate heart.

Danielle Jewhurst (11)
Four Elms Primary School, Edenbridge

Fear

Fear is grey, like a dull morning,
Fear smells like an evil smelly ogre,
Fear sounds like an ear-piercing scream,
Fear tastes like a sour lemon and lime,
Fear looks like a giant crack between two people.

Andrew Gower Ballard (10)
Four Elms Primary School, Edenbridge

Worry

Worry is blue, like butterflies in my stomach,
Worry tastes like a cold ice cube melting in my mouth,
Worry smells like fear burning into my nostrils,
Worry looks like somebody being hurt in front of me,
Worry sounds like a gigantic explosion.

Christy Mitchell (10)
Four Elms Primary School, Edenbridge

Darkness

A monster digging, crushing, roaring up your insides,
That's what darkness is.
Frozen air, solid, unhelpful and cold,
That's what darkness smells like.
Icicles freezing up your insides and body,
That's what darkness tastes like.
The sea and wind washing and blowing away your hopes and dreams
That's what darkness sounds like.
A dark pit sucking you in and keeping you there,
That's what darkness looks like!

Hannah Dewhirst (10)
Four Elms Primary School, Edenbridge

Misery

Misery is black, like a dark black hole,
sucking you to the underworld.
Misery sounds like an ear-piercing shriek,
cursing your life.
Misery smells like rotten, mouldy cheese
left in the cupboard for too long.
Misery looks like a dark, gloomy, horned monster
following you everywhere you go.
It tastes like sour milk flowing through your body.

Matthew Burton (11)
Four Elms Primary School, Edenbridge

Cats

They're furry and funny
They are great fun to play with.
Cats love to play with money,
It is music to their ears.

Some are fat,
Some like their food,
Some are silly,
Some are rude.

You see them in the pet shop
With their sweet little smiles
You know they will be out
In a little while.

I love cats, cats, cats,
Do You?

Connie Bloomfield (10)
Harrison Primary School, Fareham

Dinosaurs

Dinosaurs are so cool,
If you see one your blood will be in a pool.

T-rex are the biggest, they're very deadly,
They'll eat you in one go.
Stay away you'll be in trouble.

Dinosaurs, if you see one
Run!

Natasha Miller (10)
Harrison Primary School, Fareham

My Chocolate Poem

Chocolate is my favourite food!
I like it in a bar, a box and a jar,
I'll eat it driving in the car,
I'll eat it hanging upside down
On the climbing frame bar.
In fact, I'll eat it all the way to the nearest star!

Chocolate is my favourite food!
I'll eat it all the day,
I'll eat it at breakfast,
I'll eat it for lunch,
I'll eat it for my dinner too,
I'll eat it for the rest of my life!

Chocolate is my favourite food!
Milk chocolate is my best!
But Maltesers are great for chewing,
                  crunching and sucking!
Jelly beans are great, juicy and sweet.
Pic 'n' mix is the best!

Jashan Solanki (9)
Harrison Primary School, Fareham

Bonfire Night

On Bonfire Night,
Sparklers are very bright.
They twinkle in the night,
Mostly they're white.

When the fireworks go up,
They go *bang, bang.*
They're beautiful colours,
It sounds like they sang.

Thomas Kent (10)
Harrison Primary School, Fareham

Fireworks

On the first of November,
The fireworks lay,
Resting and waiting,
For their big day.

On the second of November,
They came out of the attic,
They're a bit rusty,
But no need to panic.

On the third of November,
We wrote a poem at school,
It's about fireworks,
I think mine's really cool.

On the fourth of November,
They came out of their box,
Everyone was excited,
I was excited lots!

On the fifth of November,
When the night's dark and starry,
Off shoot the fireworks,
And off goes the *party!*

Susan Dowell (10)
Harrison Primary School, Fareham

The Flight Path Of A Dragon - Haiku

The elegant twist
He loops the loop through the sky
That is my dragon.

Vincent Cunning (10)
Harrison Primary School, Fareham

School Rules Rap

Now this is how you should behave at school
You have six feet on the floor, dude.
Do not drink from your drink bottle,
It's rude!

When you're outside you don't kick or punch
Just play around and have fun,
And play around
Now you're done.

When you're in the library
Be quiet,
Don't run around
Just be silent.

Benjamin Kissane (10)
Harrison Primary School, Fareham

The Baboon Balloon

The baboon balloon
Is very big and bright.
He is always funny
He always loves a flight.

He has his own park
By a waterfall.
He whizzes around
But doesn't care at all.

He's red and black
And has a big nose.
He spins around
And tickles his toes!

Lara Gadsdon (10)
Harrison Primary School, Fareham

My Pets

My pet hamster

I had a pet hamster,
His name was Fluffy Bob,
We had to clean his cage a lot,
And that was a very big job.

My pet cat

I had a pet cat,
His name was Gingerbread,
We had to give him stinky food,
Which smelt like something dead.

My pet dog

I had a pet dog,
His name was Grumpy Fred,
And every night I couldn't sleep,
He wouldn't go to bed.

My pet rabbit

I had a pet rabbit,
Her name was Winnie Kins,
She had to be cleaned out,
She'd come to you when you said, *'Din-dins.'*

My pet lion

I have a pet lion,
He eats loads of food,
I don't like going near him,
As he is very rude.

Sophie Hilliker (9) & Anna Davey-Evans (10)
Harrison Primary School, Fareham

Firework Night

Fireworks, fireworks in the sky,
Like blazing rockets shooting high.
Hats, gloves and scarves, snuggle up tight,
Some little kids find it a fright.
Adults be careful when you set them off,
Don't run around or you'll get a cough.
People come from far and near,
To see the fireworks reappear.
All God's nature is hidden away,
But all the children want to play.
This is the end of my little song,
And I beg you, please don't do anything wrong!

Ryan Madden (10)
Harrison Primary School, Fareham

Picnic

We're all going on a picnic today,
but we have to go a long way.

On the way I had a bun.
When we got there we had fun.

At 12 we had our lunch,
we all went, *munch, munch!*

We have to go home now,
on the way we see a baby cow.
Moo!

Alice Jones (9)
Harrison Primary School, Fareham

Leopard

Silent as a mouse,
Sly as a fox,
Strong as a bear,
Large as you,
It's as fast as a car,
Fierce as a wolf.
So watch out before a leopard comes.

Rebecca Botham (9)
Harrison Primary School, Fareham

Kittens

Kittens are cute,
Kittens are playful.
Relaxing on the sofa,
Like little balls of fluff.
Hunting slyly for mice.

James Shayler (10)
Harrison Primary School, Fareham

My Pussy - Cinquain

My cat
Lives in a hat
And I will cuddle her
She is very furry and she's
Quite sweet!

Emma Rees (10)
Harrison Primary School, Fareham

Cool Pets

Pets are great,
Pets are cool,
They are like us all.

Pets are cool,
Pets are cool,
All of them do rule,
That's why they're cool.

Pets are noisy,
Pets are loud,
That's why they're the biggest crowd.

Pets are cool,
Pets are cool,
All of them do rule,
That's why they're cool.

Laura Colebrooke (9)
Harrison Primary School, Fareham

Something Special

Today is my sleepover,
I just can't wait.
It's my sleepover,
With my mates!

We are going to stay up late,
My mates and me.
We are going to stay up late,
And watch TV.

Now whilst we are doing that,
The boys will be asleep.
Now whilst we are doing that,
They go to sleep!

Holly Wheaton (9)
Harrison Primary School, Fareham

My World

My world is an adventure waiting to happen,
My everyday life has no pattern.
I try my hardest in all I do,
And ask for help if I need you.

My friends, they are so loyal to me,
And help me if I bang my knee.
Holly, Lauren and Hannah to name a few,
And Sarah and Emma's favourite word is *'boo'*.

After school I don't get away,
And in my mum's room only do I get to play.
We have display boards,
And in music we learn about chords!

This is my world,
I learn every day.
How I can,
Make a difference one day.

Bethan Gmitrowicz (10)
Harrison Primary School, Fareham

Monkey

Look at that monkey,
Swinging in his tree,
Why is he acting just like me?
He's cheeky, lazy and crazy,
Can he play, can he play,
Can you play, I hope not!
When you sleep you are silent,
Finally peace and quiet!

Jade Burrell (9)
Harrison Primary School, Fareham

My Pets

The frog is in the pool,
Splashing up and down,
The goldfish is in the tank,
Swimming round and round.
The stick insects in the cardboard box,
Making not a sound.

These are my pets,
My pets, my pets,
These are my pets,
The ones I have got.

My frog is called Mollie,
A hopping nice pet
And Crystal the goldfish,
Who (normally) is wet!
Climba is a stick insect
Very quiet and still,
So along with Edward's ones as well,
My pets are just so brill!

These are my pets,
My pets, my pets,
These are my pets,
The ones I have got.

Hannah Sharpe (9)
Harrison Primary School, Fareham

Football - Haiku

Football is so bad
Because everyone does hack
And it hurts so much.

Daniel Edwards (10)
Harrison Primary School, Fareham

Dogs

The dogs go to the pound,
They're treated like hounds.
We have to eat bacon and chickens and eggs,
And the cages are closed with pegs.

The floor is like butter,
When they wash it clean.
They give us horrible collars,
And they don't even have names.

Jonathon Sheppard (9)
Harrison Primary School, Fareham

School - Tanka

Everyone sits down
And listens to the teacher.
Everyone shuts up
And then gets on with their work.
Then it is lunchtime, *yum-yum.*

Fleur Gascoigne (10)
Harrison Primary School, Fareham

Who Can Tell?

A ghostly ghoul sails through,
The remains of a living room.
And who can tell what he's trying to seek,
A beautiful cheek or a mouldy leak?
Nobody will ever know,
Whether he is trying to peek,
At what I am trying to speak.

Ellen McDonald (9)
Harrison Primary School, Fareham

My Friends

First of all there's Emma,
She is really kind,
And a great laugh
And she's the best friend you can find.

Then there's Sarah-Ann,
She is really cool,
And great fun
And to be her friend you have to rule.

Next of all there's Hannah,
She is so nice,
And very kind
She has friendly mice.

After that there's Holly,
She's really fun,
And really nice,
She's as bright as the sun.

Last of all there's Bethan,
She is so great,
And pure fun,
When she comes round your house she is never late.

Lauren Taylor (9)
Harrison Primary School, Fareham

My Friend's Dog

A dog is as bouncy as a yo-yo
A dog is as daft as a peanut
A dog is as cuddly as a teddy bear
His tail wags like maracas being shaken
His blunt claws will not pierce my skin
His smile is always reassuring.

Freya Bowes (9)
Harrison Primary School, Fareham

Polly The Parrot

Polly the parrot loves food,
But hates her owner's choice,
Her owner's mean, she's not nice,
Her owner's stroppy and very uptight!

Polly is sad by what she is given,
The parrot next door gets glorious food,
She hates everything about him
But loves the delicious dishes he gets.

At night she dreams of all the food,
Marshmallows especially, those she loves
But instead she gets this gross glob,
Which makes her squawk!

Maria Roberson (9)
Harrison Primary School, Fareham

Ghost Bumps - Cinquain

The ghost
Shivers coldly
Through the ice frost window
The wind roars about it creaking
Ice-cold!

Alice Frampton (9)
Harrison Primary School, Fareham

Cats - Haiku

Cats are so, so good
Cats sleep at night-time inside
That's my cat by me.

Peter Kovacs (10)
Harrison Primary School, Fareham

Hamsters

Small as a pen, happy as can be, cute furry friends.
Nocturnal as a bat, as quick as a heartbeat.
As shy as a butterfly, dopey as a jester.
Quiet as a winter's night
But as loud as a wolf in the night.

Anna Harriman (9)
Harrison Primary School, Fareham

Monkeys

Monkey swings, leaps and plays,
Eating bananas all day.
Monkey cheeky, monkey funny,
Monkey joker of the jungle.

Abigail Fifield (9)
Harrison Primary School, Fareham

My Best Friend - Cinquain

Best friend
She is so cool
She's been my friend for years
She's so good at being my friend
It's Tash.

Chloe Llowarch 10)
Harrison Primary School, Fareham

Autumn - Tanka

Today the leaves fall
Because it is autumn now
The leaves are brownish
We now go and kick the leaves
And then put them in a pile.

Barney Richardson (10)
Harrison Primary School, Fareham

Snowflakes - Cinquain

Snowflakes
Sparkle and shine
The moonlight keeps them cool
When the sun comes in it melts them
Bye-bye.

Sydney-Rose Lawson (10)
Harrison Primary School, Fareham

Kittens - Cinquains

Kittens
Are so friendly
You can play with them lots
They're lovely to have as your pet.
Purr, purr.

Felicity Martin (9)
Harrison Primary School, Fareham

The Playground - Cinquain

I ran
In the playground
With all of my best friends
We were playing a game of 'it'
I won.

Ewen Steele (9)
Harrison Primary School, Fareham

The Blob!

If you want a fright
Switch off your light,
Because there will be the blob.
He'll give you a slob,
Slime not water
It's a slaughter.
A killer thing,
It's everything.
You will be lying dead,
On your bed.
He has a feast,
What a beast!
He scoffs you down,
As well as your gown.
He's behind your door,
Don't ask for more.
He's so vain,
Feel the pain.
People say he won't hurt a fly,
But they find out when they die.
An ankle biter,
A serious fighter.
No one has lived to tell the tale,
When he sights you, you go pale,
You'll always fail.
You wouldn't want to be belly flopped,
He's a monster that needs to be stopped.
It's only your imagination,
Death by suffocation!

Edward Spencer (10)
Haslemere Preparatory School, Haslemere

Tsunami Strikes

They say Mother Nature is powerful, let me tell you
They're correct.
I was fishing and the water started bobbling.
I said to myself, just ignore it.
A wall of water came up, I stared
Drowning, I new I was dying.

I tried to look for my wife and children
No matter, all I could see -
Dead people.
I say Satan caused it.

Gareth Jones (10)
Haslemere Preparatory School, Haslemere

Tsunami

The monstrous wall ran viciously towards me
It drew me inwards with strength no man could have
With force it came like a monstrous army with countless ranks
With swallowing and sucking it took away people's lives
Nothing could stop this monster with no heart
With destruction and death only in its mind it hit with ravenous hunger
Then the people came to see what was happening
And their life was taken away from them with no mercy.
Nature strikes.

Freddie Thomas (10)
Haslemere Preparatory School, Haslemere

Winter - Haikus

A blanket of white
Covers the ground and glistens
Swirling and twirling

Yes it is snowing
Snowball and snowmen are fun
It is settling now

In winter ice forms
On top of puddles is one
And icicles come

The end of winter
It is quite a big fright when
It drifts out of sight.

Simon Benwell (10)
Haslemere Preparatory School, Haslemere

Nature At Its Worst

Colossal and black it came out of nowhere,
Poseidon got angry and lashed out,
People scream like in a bad dream,
For their towns are dead.

People run for their very lives,
Even the bees leave their hives.
Bodies are found mostly drowned,
Families shall mourn till dawn.

Children cry, no wonder why,
Their lives are wrecked.
They look for their parents, but not much luck,
150,000 lie dead.

Toby Ward
Haslemere Preparatory School, Haslemere

The Killer Wave

The wave hit the shore
running up the beach
and through the towns,
crunching, crushing and corrupting
everything which got in its way
like a bully in a playground,
scaring everybody and
making them run for their lives
as if it was another world war.
People ran from their homes
before the wave overtook them
and drowned them.
Shrieking, screaming and screeches
were heard and people ran
like a stampede.

Tom Lowndes (11)
Haslemere Preparatory School, Haslemere

The Attic Toys

Crikey! It's dark up here
I wonder what's in this box?
Maybe a plane or a baby ox.
Hey look! A rubber toy for my cat,
Yikes! A bat!

Hey! Who would put a light bulb in a toy box?
What the? A doll with chickenpox.

What's this? I think I will take a peek,
Drip . . . drop . . . drip . . . drop
Argh! A leak.

James Bennett (9)
Haslemere Preparatory School, Haslemere

My Magic Box

(Based on 'Magic Box' by Kit Wright)

I will put in my box . . .
The cross which Jesus died on
A twig from a snowman's arm
A silk carpet from an evil witch.

I will put in my box . . .
A curly pig's tail
A slice of mouldy cheese
The inside of a conker tree.

I will put in my box . . .
A treasure chest from the bottom of a sea
A third horn of a bull
An eighth continent.

My box is fashioned from rock hard steel
And right through the middle is an orange peel
With a golden bee on every corner
A long line of ivy is its border.

I will ski in my box
On the high mountains of the Alps
I will ski down to the bottom
And hit the bottom of the box.

Johnny Taylor (10)
Haslemere Preparatory School, Haslemere

The Killer

The wave ran up the shore,
Swallowing people in its path.
There was screaming and shouting
From people and wind alike.
The wave retreated
Leaving bodies on the ground
Sand was pouring at them.
The wave hurtled up the beach
Retreating again,
Sucking the bodies with it.
People are racing the tide,
Both of which are carrying children.
A maternal murderer.
Now the sea is eating away at families.
Soon there'll be nothing left.
It is an incident that no one will forget.

Charlie van Oppen (10)
Haslemere Preparatory School, Haslemere

All Seasons

The seasons are wonderful.
Spring is when plants and
Animals grow or give birth,
In summer you can
Play on a beach or
Go outside and play.
In autumn you can play with
Leaves or stay warm.
In winter you can play in snow
Or play on something.

Jamie Bellenger (8)
Haslemere Preparatory School, Haslemere

I Love Hamsters

L ovely and cuddly
O ther people are allergic to them
V ery small feet
E veryone should like hamsters

H amsters are something that keeps you company
A hamster is small and delicate
M y brother has one and I have two
S ome people have hamsters which squeal
T hat's because they haven't been tamed
E veryone should like hamsters
R ound and round and round
S ome hamsters are snugly just like mine.

Monica Barker (9)
Haselworth Primary School, Gosport

Litter Everywhere

L itter, litter everywhere
I do not like litter
T ry not to throw litter on the floor
T oddlers can slip on litter
E veryone hates litter
R age at the people dropping litter.

L itter is very messy
I t is very slippery
T ry and pick up your own litter
T yres on cars run over litter
E veryone should pick up litter
R ed and black bottle tops can be dangerous litter.

Lucy Kendall (8)
Haselworth Primary School, Gosport

Winter

Over the land across the sea,
The seasonal winter came to see me,
Cold, cold in the winter breeze
Toes and fingers start to freeze.

Under the Atlantic Ocean,
The water jingles in slow motion,
The cloud will gather up the snow
And it zooms around the world for it to grow.

People wake up to the colour white,
They'll say, 'Snow, what a beautiful sight.'
Over the land, across the sea,
The seasonal winter came to see me.

Gemma Kingsley (9)
Haselworth Primary School, Gosport

My Cat Greyling

My cat is so friendly
Always cuddly
He tries his best
Always rests.

He's just a plain cat
He is just so fat
He has super hearing
And keeps on purring.

Dale Haste (9)
Haselworth Primary School, Gosport

Ghosts, Ghosts, Ghosts

G hosts are real sometimes and mean
H ave I seen one in the night?
O ver at that house there are ghosts
T a-ta I don't want to see them again
S oon I might see one in my room.

G hosts are transparent
H ave I seen one in the night?
O ver that hill my mum said there are ghosts
S ee that bedroom - my sister said it's haunted
T onight I have to sleep in the haunted bedroom
S o Mum said, 'Don't be scared!'

G hosts are happy in the night
H ave ghosts been in these rooms?
O ver there, there are ghosts
S ee - they hide
T onight it will be scary
S ee that morning I will stay in my bed.

Emma Churcher (10)
Haselworth Primary School, Gosport

Football Is Cool

Football is cool, with the ball
Football is good, no matter the weather
All the players working together
The crowds enjoying themselves no matter the score
Goals coming in, more and more
All the teams playing their best
Even if the ref's a pest!

David Martin (10)
Haselworth Primary School, Gosport

Matt Jay

I love Matt Jay from Busted!

L ove is in the air
O ver the moon I will jump
V ery much in love
E very song I love

M att is my hero
A nd he's the best
T hinks he's a good skateboarder
T hat's not quite true, yet -

J affa cakes he does not like
A nd he's the best -
Y oga is not his favourite thing.

Sophie Davies (10)
Haselworth Primary School, Gosport

Sunny Days

S unny days eating a peach
U nusual days are today
M aking sandcastles on the beach
M erry days to remember
E very day I wish to be like this
R eams of ideas to tell Miss.

Sunny mornings, sunny afternoons
Lovely days swimming in a pool
Mum calls us for dinner
First one finished is the winner
Tired children go to bed
Brushing off the excitement for tomorrow.

Shannon Leary (10)
Haselworth Primary School, Gosport

Dogs Are Cooler Than Humans

D ogs are clever
O f any kind
G et away, dogs will follow
S ometimes dogs are great

A nd when they are trained
R ight paw, left paw, both paws too
E very, everywhere is she?

C assey, Cassey, where are you?
O n and on - where is she?
O ver the world - where is she?
L et's go out and find her
E nd now, end, please come home
R are and cold, where are you?

T hat is where you are!
H ello she barks and there are some puppies
A nd when she is found at home
N ever runs away again.

H appy, happy you are here
U nder my bed
M y dog is safe at home
A nd there you are, stay in your bed
N ever ever run away again
S leep, sleep, go to sleep and wake up in the morning.

Sian Bowles (9)
Haselworth Primary School, Gosport

Spring

Spring, spring, nice and cool,
Kids and adults playing basketball,
Lots of flowers big and bright,
They're always here, all day and night.

Spring is my favourite season,
For that I have no reason,
Spring is lush, spring is cool,
It wouldn't be spring without a paddling pool.

Lots of pretty flowers,
Which are here all twenty-four hours,
Lots of pretty colours here,
Which go all the way up to the pier.

Kelly Deacon (10)
Haselworth Primary School, Gosport

My Hamster

Snoozing snugly in his nest,
Always trying to be his best,
If you touch his pink, little nose,
He will always try to do a pose.

If you see him in his wheel,
Cover your ears cos he might squeal,
If you see him in the ball,
Watch out cos he'll hit the wall.

If you see his little smile,
You'll want to hold him for a while,
If you put him in his bowl,
You'll feel as if he's touched your soul.

Kiera Kingsley (10)
Haselworth Primary School, Gosport

PlayStations

P layStations are fun
L ying around and playing
A nd sitting down on the bed and the floor
Y ou can drive cars and talk to people
S itting on the floor can give you pins and needles
T alking to other people in Final Fantasy
A nd gathering other people in Final Fantasy
T ill it is the end and you have to start again unless you save it half
   way through
I t's sometimes annoying when it does not work
O n some days it does not load, but it is good when it does
N ow you know all about PlayStations and now it is time to
S ay bye-bye!

Kyle Taylor (9)
Haselworth Primary School, Gosport

Play Up Pompey

P ompey is the best
O ur team rules
M anagers need rests
P ompey think Southampton are fools
E xcellent team is Pompey
Y akubu is the best player in history.

Harley Faulkes (8)
Haselworth Primary School, Gosport

The Human Body

The human body is like a big science lab gone wrong
The heart is a stress ball
The small intestines are a tangled ball of wool
The brain is a computer memory
The muscles are like the icing on a cake
The skeleton is a mass of sticks in a bag
The eyes are like a window into another world
The skin is a bag containing Nik-Naks
The systems are like a factory of pipes and bags
The nose is a big carrot
The ears are like butterfly wings
The belly is a big hot cross bun
The mouth is like a speaker
The hand is a big glove
The skull is like a giant turtle shell
The bladder is a big whoopee cushion
The hair is like a plant growing wild
The head is a big, colourful ball.

Danielle Hands (10)
Malden Parochial Primary School, Worcester Park

The Human Body

My blood rushes round my body,
Racing like athletes round the track

My heart pumps and beats,
Like a drum player beating a rhythm

My liver cleans my blood,
Like the way I wash myself

My lungs inflate and deflate,
Like a balloon being blown up and let down

Food falls down my intestine,
Like me going on a roller coaster.

Katie Holland (10)
Malden Parochial Primary School, Worcester Park

The Human Body

Skin as pink as a peach newly picked
Grazes happen, scraping the skin when I fall over
Like a baby which hasn't taken its first footstep
Ears at the side of our head so we can hear
Like a cheetah from miles away
Feet so we can walk like a model gracefully
Eyes so we can see
Like a bird catching its prey
A tongue so we can taste the juiciness
Like freshly picked fruit
Noses so we can smell the loveliness of our warm dinners
Hands so we can feel our pet's fur
Like a blanket in bed
Fingers so we can scratch out irritations
Like a cat
Our body is useful so it can cure itself, its own doctor.

Our heart so we can live our lives
Like a tortoise can
Our lungs pumping blood in and out
Like a balloon pump
Our skeleton so we're not floppy
Like a piece of worn out paper
Our muscles so we can become fit
Like a workout instructor
Our brain so we can think like a science genius
The inside of our body so we can live
Like an animal on the planet.

Jessica Partleton (10)
Malden Parochial Primary School, Worcester Park

The Human Body

The human body is a giant burning fireball
It circulates the blood round and round
Here comes the oxygen in through my mouth
In through the veins, down to the heart
Now the arteries are here to take over
Up, down and round my body and back up to my mouth
Once again I breathe in the air as sweet as syrup.

The potato is giving energy
And is entered through my mouth where all is being churned
                                                    up into little balls
Down deep they roll into my stomach where juices are being poured in
Now into my intestines all wiggly and swirly, like new sausages
Down the mushed up food falls into my anus
I need the toilet!

My front teeth are made to cut up food
And my side teeth are there to shred up food
So lastly the molars will grind and chew
Spit helps to make your food slippery so it can slide down your throat
When I was little I had twenty teeth
But now I'm older I have thirty-two teeth.

Vicky Stanton (11)
Malden Parochial Primary School, Worcester Park

The Human Body Poem

My heart is like a tennis ball pumping constantly
My ribcage is like bits of steel protecting my lungs
If I had no bones in my body I would be as floppy as jelly
If I had no skull I would be as squidgy as a marshmallow
My hair is like grass growing faster and faster
My eyes are as brown as rich dark chocolate
My legs are as fast as a race horse's.

Max Edwards (10)
Malden Parochial Primary School, Worcester Park

The Human Body

The human body is a work of art
It has complicated parts working all day long
Its long bones stretch far
With tiny bones which are like needles.

Organs which are longer than two miles
A clever organ which is the brain
Better than any computer.

It has a structure like a building
The skeleton is as white as an albino cow
And it has joints like a hinge.

The human body is like a robot
It's clever
It's fantastic
There is nothing else like it.

Jordan Yardley (11)
Malden Parochial Primary School, Worcester Park

The Human Body

Let's start off with the head
My head is full of ideas, it is a human computer
My ears are for hearing
My nose is for smelling things from flowers to candles
My eyes are big and brown and owl-like
My mouth is for eating and my teeth are for chewing
They are as white and shiny as pearls
My arms are for many things, they are as stretchy as elastic bands
My hands are wriggly and fast like spiders
My tummy stores all my chewed food and is like a mini pantry
My legs are as long as ladders and are very speedy too
My feet are for walking on
And are as nimble and delicate as a ballerina
Overall my whole body is as flexible and strong as a giant rubber.

Vanessa Mundy (11)
Malden Parochial Primary School, Worcester Park

The Human Body

Your brain is like a ball of seaweed
Your eyes are marbles rolling round and round
The ear is the letter 'C' hovering on your head
And your lips are red rose petals moving on your face
The heart is a blood-red apple sitting in your body
And your lungs are two rugby balls
Your liver is like a snail's shell
And your kidneys are two eyes looking inside your body
Your stomach is a carrier bag tied at the handles
The bladder is a CD with two wires coming out of it
Your muscles are lots of fingerprints
And your skeleton is a lot of big and small doggy bones.

Your head is a disco ball always moving round and round
Your neck is a pencil pot with a ball on top
The chest is a beanbag
And your bottom is a peach
Your arms are like snakes on the side of your chest
Your hands are like claws always clinging onto something
The legs are a pair of long stilts
And your feet are a pair of flatfish at the end of your legs, not the sea!

Rachel Martin (10)
Malden Parochial Primary School, Worcester Park

Human Body Poem

The heart is like a big tennis ball
Hitting the floor several times
My eyes, big and round, like a shiny diamond
My teeth are like knives cutting the food
My skeleton has big, strong bones
When they are broken they start to groan
Your blood is racing against the clock to get to the finish line
On your body you have lots of hairs,
They're all different colours, black, brown and bare
The human body is a strange thing, it can run, jump and sing.

Luke Jackson (10)
Malden Parochial Primary School, Worcester Park

Human Body Poem

The human body is like a robot
The heart is like the fuse making it work
The brain is like a control pad telling it what to do
The veins are like wires taking the electricity
The robot has a face letting out emotions like we do
The eyes are like flashing headlights when they see.

The robots have sensors like our mouths and ears
They are being told what to do, just like us
The hands are like claws on long poles
The feet are like metal plates with stone-cold soles
The intestine is just a box full of wires
The liver holds it all together
This it what the human body is like
When you are a robot.

Patrick Redmond (10)
Malden Parochial Primary School, Worcester Park

The Human Body

Our veins are like the sewage system
Long winding pipes all over the place,
Bones are like long white bricks
Keeping us up and strong all the time
Blood flows like water through a stream
Legs move us like wheels move a car
The heart keeps us going like an engine
Pumping fluids throughout the body.
Our liver cleans out our blood removing any infection
No one knows exactly how the brain works
An unbreakable lock that will never pour out its secrets,
Ligaments and muscles pull and stretch like elastic bands
Arms move and pick up things like two cranes.

Lewis McCormack (10)
Malden Parochial Primary School, Worcester Park

The Human Body

I had a patient in theatre once
Who had a punctured lung
I stuck my hand inside the body
A vein got stuck round my thumb.

The heart was small and red
The lung was flat and like a pear
The liver was like a snail
And the stomach was a bag of air.

The pair of kidneys like some eyes
The intestines were spaghetti
The brain a lump of seaweed
My insides are not pretty.

Although I could tussle with my muscle
I had myself to blame
Although my bones are all my own
I really am quite tame.

Heather Martin (10)
Malden Parochial Primary School, Worcester Park

The Human Body

Your brain is like a wriggling worm
Your eyes are like an egg
Your heart is like an apple pumping up and down
Your hair is like a big, puffy koala bear
Your bones are like Nik-Naks
Your throat is like a gurgling grape
Your blood is like tomato ketchup
Your ribs are like a big, bony gate.

Ben Jones (10)
Malden Parochial Primary School, Worcester Park

The Human Body

The human body is a funny thing
The heart beats like a thumping hand
It's made up of cells like orange bits
Our eyeballs are stretchy like an elastic band
Which bends around and is sticky.

We have to breathe so we've got our lungs
The lungs, the lungs get all the oxygen
And gets rid of carbon dioxide
Our ears can hear things like a sound wave
Our kidneys clear all the dirt and takes it down to the
Waste and out of the body.

You won't see your bones till you're dead
Let's start with your head, your skull is rock hard
It's a bodyguard to your brain
It might hurt if you bang your head
But you will still live.

Your ribs protect your heart and lungs
You need your ribcage to protect them
If you don't have one, if you injure yourself
You will die.

Without our pelvis we cannot walk
Because there would be nothing to hang our legs on
Without a skeleton we would be all floppy
So that's why I'm the captain of the human body.

Christopher Herbert (10)
Malden Parochial Primary School, Worcester Park

Hosts Of Darkness

'I'm back from war!' said the red cloaked soldier,
Banging on the sunset door.
From the silence came the snorting of his horse
As it sniffed the dandelions and daisies.
Fluttering, a golden bird flew from the chimney
Silhouetting itself in the flame-red sun.
He gave another drowsy knock for the second time,
'It's me, I'm home!'
But still nobody appeared at the oak door.
No jewel-eyed child or woman from the glacier window
Peered into his lost blue eyes,
Where he stood motionless and rigid.
But only a family of frozen souls that haunted the lifeless house,
Then hovered listening in the amber sunlight
To the calling that once belonged to their hearts,
Stood thronging the bright ruby sunbeams on the light stair,
That leads down the unloved, empty hall,
Heartening in a dust stirred sleep
By the lost soldier's call.

Lily Johnson (10)
Mereworth CP School, Mereworth

It's Just The Wolf

'What's that creature that hides stealthily in the darkness?'
'Sshh, it's just the wolf.'

'What's stalking the forest and killing any animal it sees?'
'Sshh, it's just the wolf.'

'What's darting on the ground like a mad dog,
Biting its enemies and howling at the moon?'

'Sshh, my dearest, it's just the wolf,
Killing in the darkness till its appetite is pleased.
Sshh, my dearest, it's just the wolf,
When you're eating in the morning, it will be no more.'

Tom Cuttle (11)
Mereworth CP School, Mereworth

The Moody Teacher

What shall we do with a moody teacher?
What shall we do with a moody teacher?
What shall we do with a moody teacher
Early in the morning?

Make her squirm with a worm in her plimsolls,
Attack her with the blown up netballs,
Make her afraid of all the pupils
Early in the morning.

Please Miss we're only kidding,
How come your legs are skidding?
Is that our graves you're digging
Early in the morning?

What shall we do with a moody teacher?
What shall we do with a moody teacher?
What shall we do with a moody teacher
Early in the morning?

Should we give him a detention
So he can pay attention?
No, maybe a suspension
Early in the morning.

Please Sir we're only lying,
Oh no, do stop crying,
Is that our hands you're tying,
Early in the morning?

What shall we do with a moody teacher?
What shall we do with a moody teacher?
What shall we do with a moody teacher,
Early in the morning?

Make her sit on a great big hedgehog,
Leave her alone with a vicious dog,
Force her to clean out the bogs,
Early in the morning!

Hannah Bond (10)
Mereworth CP School, Mereworth

Nothing Is There

She imagined she heard
A flapping on the stair,
'It's nothing,' she whispered,
'Nothing is there.'
She thought then she heard
A hooting in the hall,
'It's nothing,' she said again,
'It's nothing at all.'
But she didn't decide to open the door
In case she found nothing
Standing there
On a branch, or in armour, or with a claw.
Frighteningly quiet she was stuck to her seat
While nothing roamed the house
On great big feet,
But it was strange though
And she noticed this,
When on her own before
Nothing flew throughout the house,
But never through the door.
The answer, she thought,
Was very easy,
It was because there was nothing there -
Again!

George Campbell (10)
Mereworth CP School, Mereworth

The Grumpy Dad!

What shall we do with the grumpy dad?
What shall we do with the grumpy dad?
What shall we do with the grumpy dad
Early in the morning?

Tie him up behind the cupboard door,
Turn him upside down on the kitchen floor,
Lock him up in a busy store,
Early in the morning.

Please Dad, I'm only teasing,
Don't mean to be displeasing,
But I am just being enterprising,
Early in the morning.

What shall we do with the grumpy dad?
What shall we do with the grumpy dad?
What shall we do with the grumpy dad
Early in the morning?

Stand him outside in the cold rain,
Do something naughty and say he was the one to blame,
Tell him he is a pain,
Early in the morning.

Please Dad, I'm only kidding,
I thought you weren't listening,
Ouch - that's my head you're squeezing,
Early in the morning.

What shall we do with the grumpy dad?
What shall we do with the grumpy dad?
What shall we do with the grumpy dad
Early in the morning?

Melanie Cuddon (10)
Mereworth CP School, Mereworth

The Followers . . .

(Inspired by 'The Listeners' by Walter de la Mare)

As the traveller rode away
Across the forest's moonlit floor
There was a soft and timid creak
Of the opening of a door.
And out of the moonlight
Behind the traveller's head
Glided hundreds of ghostly figures
The phantoms of the *dead!*
The traveller stopped dead in his tracks
As his horse whinnied and cried
It had sensed an awesome presence -
A presence of which had died.
The forest turned an icy-blue -
Different to its luscious green
As wherever the dead lingered
Came winter which had been.
And now the traveller contemplated hard
And then he thought he knew
The cause of the forest's icy feel -
To turn a frosty blue.
Aye, the phantoms followed the traveller
Through the heart of the unfriendly wood
And then he said to himself
'If only they'd stayed in their domains,
If only they could . . .'

Ben Edmonds (10)
Mereworth CP School, Mereworth

The Shop Assistant

What shall we do with the shop assistant?
What shall we do with the shop assistant?
What shall we do with the shop assistant
Early in the morning?

Hang her on the meat hook where people can see her,
Put her on the conveyor belt and scan her,
Polish all the floors up all shiny with her
Early in the morning.

Please Miss, we're only kidding,
Don't start the food a-skidding,
For all you, we'll be bidding
Early in the morning.

What shall we do with the shop assistant?
What shall we do with the shop assistant?
What shall we do with the shop assistant
Early in the morning?

Send her out to do the trolleys in the snowfall,
Keep her long hours after work to have a role call,
Make her reach the highest shelf because she is small
Early in the morning.

Please Miss, we're only joking,
How come your face is smoking?
Ouch - that's us you're poking
Early in the morning.

What shall we do with the shop assistant?
What shall we do with the shop assistant?
What shall we do with the shop assistant
Early in the morning?

Throw a nut at her massive, fat belly,
Drop her in the fish to make her more smelly,
Put her on a till to be a shop assistant
Early in the morning.

Jessica Calderwood (10)
Mereworth CP School, Mereworth

Ruby

Shining softly, the sun silently appears,
Now replacing the moon.
Glistening on everything she sees and watches,
Ruby leaves on burgundy trees.
As the sun catches the compact cottage,
Showing ruby windows with a ruby glint,
Laying in his kennel like a hog,
With paw of ruby, leaps out the dog.
From the shadowy trees the scarlet breast peeps
Of the robin in a ruby-feathered wake.
A silent spider scurries by,
With ruby fangs and ruby eyes,
And motionless frogs in the water gleam
By ruby reeds in the ruby stream.

Sarah Loines (10)
Mereworth CP School, Mereworth

Golden Sun

Slowly, silently now the sun sinks,
Smoothly gliding through the night sky.
She peered this way and that and saw,
Golden leaves upon golden trees.
One by one the windows clutched her beams
Beneath the thatched golden roof.
Asleep in his kennel like a plank of wood,
With a coat like a golden cloak.
From their gloomy cotte, white-breasted peep,
Of doves in golden feathers sleep.
A harvest mouse scuttles by,
With golden claws and golden eyes.
And motionless fish in the waters gleam,
By golden reeds in a golden stream.

Zoe Moore (11)
Mereworth CP School, Mereworth

Annoying Sister

What shall we do with the annoying sister?
What shall we do with the annoying sister?
What shall we do with the annoying sister
Early in the morning?

Never lets me use her mobile phone
Speaks to me in a grumpy tone
All she does is moan, moan, moan
Early in the morning.

Her hair is always in a mess
She never wears a pretty dress
She's like Nessie from Loch Ness
Early in the morning.

What shall we do with the annoying sister?
What shall we do with the annoying sister?
What shall we do with the annoying sister
Early in the morning?

She never does what she is told
Always wears lots of gold
I do wish that she was sold
Early in the morning.

She's always looking in the mirror
When she shouts it makes me quiver
And my body starts to shiver
Early in the morning.

What shall we do with the annoying sister?
What shall we do with the annoying sister?
What shall we do with the annoying sister
Early in the morning?

Lauren Smith (10)
Mereworth CP School, Mereworth

Bald Headmaster

What shall we do with a bald headmaster?
What shall we do with a bald headmaster?
What shall we do with a bald headmaster
Early in the morning?

Polish his head with the cleaner's duster,
Trying to avoid the moley cluster,
Then his head will have a brighter lustre,
Early in the morning.

Sorry Sir, we didn't mean it,
We just thought we ought to clean it,
Oh my word, you should have seen it,
Early in the morning.

What shall we do with a bald headmaster?
What shall we do with a bald headmaster?
What shall we do with a bald headmaster
Early in the morning?

This curly wig will update your look,
It only falls off when your head is shook,
There are other styles in the catalogue book
Early in the morning.

Honest Sir, it looks quite cool,
Go on wear it in to school,
It looks better than our gruel
Early in the morning.

What shall we do with a bald headmaster?
What shall we do with a bald headmaster?
What shall we do with a bald headmaster
Early in the morning?

We've measured it to be a perfect fit,
We're certain Sir, it's got no nits,
They're just little brown wriggly bits,
Early in the morning.

William Ashworth (11)
Mereworth CP School, Mereworth

White

Slowly, crisply, the white snow hardens,
This way and that it covers the gardens;
I look upon the white cold trees,
And see the branches in the breeze.
The birds have flown to warmer places,
And children play with icy-pinched faces.
Crouched in its bed like a rat,
With a white coat, sleeps the cat;
From the depth of the snow the white coat peeps,
Of a polar bear in an ice cold sleep.
A red squirrel goes scampering by,
With snow-white claws and crystal-white eyes.
A clear white fish hangs motionless in the frozen stream,
With cloud white ice with a gleam.

Heidi Beaven (10)
Mereworth CP School, Mereworth

Golden

Glistening, gleaming now the golden trees,
With a golden trunk and golden leaves.
This way and that, she peered and she saw,
A golden lily hanging from the golden door.
Shining windows reflecting against the light,
Now the sky was dark and inky, it was night.
Asleep in his kennel, as still as a log,
With fur of golden, lies the dog.
A diminutive squirrel goes scampering past,
With claws of golden and eyes of glass,
And motionless fish in the water gleam,
By golden reeds and a golden stream.

Abigail McCarthy (10)
Mereworth CP School, Mereworth

The Gel Crazy Boy

What shall we do with the gel crazy boy?
What shall we do with the gel crazy boy?
What shall we do with the gel crazy boy
Early in the morning.

Steal all his gel and replace it with 'pink hell',
When he tries it out he'll yell and yell,
Then I'll match him up with a pink crazy girl,
Early in the morning.

Please boy, I'm only laughing,
Don't be so harsh, you're a daft thing,
All you need is a bit of 'bling',
Early in the morning.

What shall we do with the gel crazy boy?
What shall we do with the gel crazy boy?
What shall we do with the gel crazy boy
Early in the morning.

Style your hair like a great baboon,
Show it off in class and the girls will swoon,
Start a rap to an Eminem tune,
Early in the morning.

Please boy, stop it now,
We can't stand the row,
Everyone evacuate to Maidstone Town,
Early in the morning.

What shall we do with the gel crazy boy?
What shall we do with the gel crazy boy?
What shall we do with the gel crazy boy
Early in the morning.

Bring him back to school all posh and clean,
Show him to the headmaster, he won't scream,
He'll think his hair has a lovely sheen,
Early in the morning.

Laura Edmonds (10)
Mereworth CP School, Mereworth

Watching, Listening

(Inspired by 'The Listeners' by Walter de la Mare)

'Let me come in,' shouted the man dressed in black,
Thumping on the dusty door;
His horse stood in peace, enjoying eating scruffily
At the forgotten grass of the palace garden's restful floor:
Suddenly a blackbird soared out of the chimney,
Sweeping over the man's head.
He took another hit to the door a second time;
'Let me enter my home,' he said.
But no one opened the dusky door to the black man;
No one sat on the unswept sill
Or even peered over and gazed into his large green eyes,
Where the man dressed in black stood perplexed and still.
But the only creatures that were there, were a host of phantom
Listeners that dwelt together in the magnificent palace
Who sat watching, listening in the quiet of the moon
From the voice of the world of men:
Sat thronging as light swept over them on the grandiose staircase,
That revealed the insubstantial hall,
Hearing voices that have been whisked and smoothed
By the magical black man's call.
But suddenly he felt strange inside,
The watchers were answering his questions and his cry,
Meanwhile his horse walked and at the same time ate
The delicious turf, underneath the black and silver sky
He then banged on the distant door, even harder, he lifted his head -
'Please say to them I came to talk to them, but no one let me in,
Tell them that I kept my promise,' he said.
The watchers and the listeners made no movement,
Although every word the black man spoke
Fell, echoing through the still, grand palace,
The echo came from the only human left awake in the village:
Aye, they heard him canter off to find a new home,
And the sight of his black hat falling rapidly to the ground,
But how he left his beloved family behind,
They could never see him again.

Holly Burgess (11)
Mereworth CP School, Mereworth

The Listeners

(Inspired by 'The Listeners' by Walter de la Mare)

'Are you there?' called the traveller,
Tapping on the starlit door;
His horse leant against the bare winter's tree
Eating old leaves off the floor;
Bats squeaked as the light shone in their dark eyes,
The traveller heard them ahead,
He knocked harder, much harder the second time;
'Is anyone there?' he said wondering,
Still no one unlocked the bolted door,
No hand opened the curtain left on the window sill,
Stared out to look at his lonely face,
Standing there leaning against the door, still,
But only a host of phantom spirits listened
That were grounded together, then,
Stood watching from the bedroom window,
To help the man's soul from the world of men
Waiting, the air had been shaken, by what?
Shaken by the traveller's call,
He knew in his heart they were strangers,
Soundless screams answered his cry,
A cloud swayed and covered the moon,
No light rays appeared from the sky,
He rattled against the door;
They squealed, he lifted his head,
'I came, I kept my word, see I am true,
But no one answered,' he said.
But still nothing stirred the listeners, too
Though the words he spoke
Swiftly his words flew down the endless hall
From the only thing left awake
The sound of iron to stone
Hooves went in the distance
Fading in the wind of the sea.

Rebecca Leong (10)
Mereworth CP School, Mereworth

The Science Teacher!

What shall we do with the science teacher?
What shall we do with the science teacher?
What shall we do with the science teacher
Early in the morning?

Invent a new potion direct from the ocean
Seaweed and sand will complete the promotion
Market it well and see the commotion
Early in the morning.

Please Sir, don't be boring
Buy some more, it's so adoring
The smell is sweet and the women will come pouring
Early in the morning.

What shall we do with the science teacher?
What shall we do with the science teacher?
What shall we do with the science teacher
Early in the morning?

Make him go to a training day
Make him take us to Norfolk Bay
We wish he had a mouth of clay
Early in the morning.

Please Sir, we know you're talking
I'm so tired you're walking
Oh no! You think I'm detention stalking
Early in the morning.

What shall we do with the science teacher?
What shall we do with the science teacher?
What shall we do with the science teacher
Early in the morning?

Leave him with an unidentified creature
Lock him in the lab where it can reach him
Bring him out to be a science teacher
Early in the morning.

Lauren Hare (10)
Mereworth CP School, Mereworth

The Bouncy Dog

What shall we do with the bouncy dog?
What shall we do with the bouncy dog?
What shall we do with the bouncy dog
Early in the morning?

Put him in a hole where the worms can eat him
Tie his legs up to his chest
Make him eat a chicken breast
Early in the morning.

Please Stig, we are only joking
Can't we ever stop you poking?
How come you are always soaking
Early in the morning?

What shall we do with the bouncy dog?
What shall we do with the bouncy dog?
What shall we do with the bouncy dog
Early in the morning?

Take him to a cage and leave him in it
Take him to a parents' evening
Feed him food and watch him eating
Early in the morning.

Please Stig, we were only teasing
We did not mean to keep you sneezing
Help, that's my bum you're teething,
Early in the morning.

What shall we do with the bouncy dog?
What shall we do with the bouncy dog?
What shall we do with the bouncy dog
Early in the morning?

Tickle his nose with a lump of pepper
Put him in a bag of feathers
Bring him back to the house forever
Early in the morning.

George Tye (10)
Mereworth CP School, Mereworth

What Shall We Do With The Annoying Brother?

What shall we do with the annoying brother?
What shall we do with the annoying brother?
What shall we do with the annoying brother
Early in the morning?

Smack him on the bottom to make it sore,
Lock him in the shed 'cause he's such a bore,
Take him to court 'cause he breaks the law,
Early in the morning.

Please bro, we're only playing,
Don't mean to be delaying,
Why do you keep complaining
Early in the morning?

What shall we do with the annoying brother?
What shall we do with the annoying brother?
What shall we do with the annoying brother
Early in the morning?

Give him chores to keep him busy,
Take no notice if he gets in a tizzy,
Watch him get tired and dizzy,
Early in the morning.

Please bro, we're only joking,
Don't mean to be provoking,
Help - that's my leg you're squishing,
Early in the morning.

What shall we do with the annoying brother?
What shall we do with the annoying brother?
What shall we do with the annoying brother
Early in the morning?

Frighten him with a big black spider,
Make sure he's not a survivor,
Bring him back to be an annoying brother,
Early in the morning.

Rebecca Sampson (10)
Mereworth CP School, Mereworth

The Football Player

What shall we do with the football player?
What shall we do with the football player?
What shall we do with the football player
Early in the morning?

Stop him from scoring a goal,
Like they do with Andy Cole,
Be careful not to fall down a hole,
Early in the morning.

His name is midfielder David Beckham,
He likes to play a game called Tekken,
He originally lived at London, Peckham,
Early in the morning.

What shall we do with the football player?
What shall we do with the football player?
What shall we do with the football player
Early in the morning?

What about legend goalkeeper Gordon Banks,
He performed in a final so we should say thanks,
He'd like to be placed top of the ranks,
Early in the morning.

I liked defender Ferdinand,
He used to play football for West Ham,
Now he's liked by Manchester United fans,
Early in the morning.

What shall we do with the football player?
What shall we do with the football player?
What shall we do with the football player
Early in the morning?

Great defender Gareth Southgate,
He is always punctual, never late,
Especially when his child has a school fête,
Early in the morning.

Christopher Allen (11)
Mereworth CP School, Mereworth

Monday Morning Blues

What shall we do with the boring teacher?
What shall we do with the boring teacher?
What shall we do with the boring teacher
On a Monday morning?

Try to wind her up by forgetting our homework,
Try to pull a sickie by saying I'm going to throw up,
Watch her pull her hair out before it is nine o'clock
On a Monday morning.

Please Miss, I'm only kidding,
You know me I'm only fibbing,
Try to be a bit more forgiving
On a Monday morning.

What shall we do with the geography teacher?
What shall we do with the geography teacher?
What shall we do with the geography teacher
On a Monday morning?

Pack her on a coach and take her somewhere,
Where the wind howls to mess up her hair,
To get our own back when she is being unfair,
On a Monday morning.

Please Miss, you really scare me,
When you are wailing like a banshee,
Just chill out and have a cup of tea,
On a Monday morning.

What shall we do with the science teacher?
What shall we do with the science teacher?
What shall we do with the science teacher
On a Monday morning?

Fill up her desk with moths and spiders,
Watch them swoop round her head like gliders,
I apologise for my evil ideas
On a Monday morning.

Georgia Dallas (10)
Mereworth CP School, Mereworth

The Old Headmaster

What shall we do with the old headmaster?
What shall we do with the old headmaster?
What shall we do with the old headmaster,
Early in the morning?

Lock him up in the filing drawer,
Tie him down in the PE store,
Feed him cold school dinners for evermore,
Early in the morning.

Sir, you are looking sneaky,
Why are you acting freaky,
Don't mean to be cheeky,
Early in the morning.

What shall we do with the old headmaster?
What shall we do with the old headmaster?
What shall we do with the old headmaster,
Early in the morning?

Stick his head in a smelly bin,
Make him sit on a drawing pin,
After school keep him in,
Early in the morning.

Sorry if I'm being rude,
Just in a funny mood,
Ouch - that's my ear being chewed,
Early in the morning.

What shall we do with the old headmaster?
What shall we do with the old headmaster?
What shall we do with the old headmaster,
Early in the morning?

Sian Fenn (10)
Mereworth CP School, Mereworth

Grumpy Grandad

What shall we do with the grumpy grandad?
What shall we do with the grumpy grandad?
What shall we do with the grumpy grandad
Early in the morning?

Throw him in the van for hours,
Making sure he sends Nan's flowers,
Dress him up in funny trousers,
I'll laugh all day and night.

Now he's off to Nanny's party,
And he wants to dress real tarty,
But Nanny makes him dress so smartly,
In the afternoon.

What shall we do with the grumpy grandad?
What shall we do with the grumpy grandad?
What shall we do with the grumpy grandad
Early in the morning?

Grandad's had a beer or two,
So he dashes to the loo,
Then he finds a great big queue,
Ohhh, what shall we do?

He gets humpy straight away,
Wants to get all his own way,
Try to get Nan to obey,
In the afternoon.

What shall we do with the grumpy grandad?
What shall we do with the grumpy grandad?
What shall we do with the grumpy grandad
Early in the morning?

Lose him in the woods for ages,
Try to get him grumpy babies,
Then he gets the grump for ages,
In the afternoon.

Grandad gets away real quick,
Then he really takes the mick,
Starts to call me Mrs Lick,
'Cause I licked the chocolates.

What shall we do with the grumpy grandad?
What shall we do with the grumpy grandad?
What shall we do with the grumpy grandad?
Pack him off to bed!

Hollie Dixson (10)
Mereworth CP School, Mereworth

Something!

I thought I saw
A pair of ghastly eyes,
'There's something there,' I told myself,
'There's something there.'
I thought then I saw
Two hairy feet amble towards me,
'There's something there,' I said again,
'There's something there.'
But I dare not open the door
In case I found something,
Lurking there,
'There's something there,' I repeated,
'There's something there.'
But then I realised, it was only Dad
Walking in his sleep -
Again!

Ryan Pass (11)
Mereworth CP School, Mereworth

The Grumpy Father

What shall we do with the grumpy father?
What shall we do with the grumpy father?
What shall we do with the grumpy father
Early in the morning?

Lock him in the office all day
He can moan but there he'll stay
If he moans he'll get no pay
Early in the morning.

Sorry Dad, I'm only joking
I didn't mean to get you soaking
Stop it that's my eye you're poking
Early in the morning.

What shall we do with the grumpy father?
What shall we do with the grumpy father?
What shall we do with the grumpy father
Early in the morning?

It's even worse now he's on a diet
Eating and drinking kept him quiet
Put him to sleep or there'll be a riot
Early in the morning.

When Spurs lose he's really grumpy
If Arsenal win he's twice as humpy
That happens most weeks, humpy grumpy,
Early in the morning.

What shall we do with the grumpy father?
What shall we do with the grumpy father?
What shall we do with the grumpy father
Early in the morning?

Sorry Dad, I'm only teasing
I don't mean to be displeasing
Stop! That's my neck you're squeezing
Early in the morning.

Nathan Kiddie (10)
Mereworth CP School, Mereworth

What's There?

I sensed I saw
Something under the bed
'What's there?' I asked myself
'What's there?'
I was almost certain that
There was something there
I moved a bit closer and shouted
'Who's there, or
What's there?'
But I did not turn on the light
I thought it would disappear
'What's there?' I bellowed
'What's there?'
I froze on the spot
As the thing started to move
Slithering around like
A confused worm thinking
Where am I?
What's there?
What is there?
It was bizarre though
And this had come to my mind
That, whenever alone in the dark
I'd see him every time
He'd scare me half to death
But this time he was mine
I went to turn on the light
And he started to fade away
Still to this day I wonder,
What was there?

George Farrington (10)
Mereworth CP School, Mereworth

Golden

Beautiful golden is the dawn,
On the glowing golden corn.
The golden sun sails through the sky,
Shining golden up on high.
Glowing on the straw of thatch,
The golden beams, the window's catch.
A tiny bird goes flying by,
Across a blue and golden sky.
A horse is grazing by the stream,
That glitters with a golden gleam.
But the golden dawn does not last,
For the rest of the day approaches fast.

Lorna Crease (10)
Mereworth CP School, Mereworth

The Sorrow Child

I found her you know,
All there snuggled up in her bed,
I picked her up all cold and stiff,
Tears rolled down my cheek and onto her,
I put her in a box with her belongings
And buried her with a kiss of love,
I found her you know,
I told her I would never forget her.

Claire Birchall (11)
Merlin Primary School, Bromley

Fudge

(Dedicated to my cat Fudge)

My cat Fudge is a big ginger fluff ball,
She's very energetic and runs about,
She likes to run around outside and play with her friend Cheeky.
She's always making a fuss when it comes to cat food,
Though she doesn't like milk at all,
She doesn't like chicken,
And she's not that keen on fish,
I say that she makes too much of a fuss.
Mum wanted to tell me some news later on that day,
'We've got a kitten, Rolo,' said Mum.
I put my hands over my face!

Amber Simmonds (11)
Merlin Primary School, Bromley

What Am I?

A puddle - maker
A pavement - hitter
A window - splasher
A plant - grower
A fire - destroyer
A clothes soaker
Do you know what I am?
I'm rain!

Danielle Campion (11)
Merlin Primary School, Bromley

I Forgot!

The classroom was darker than ever,
The books cast a shadowy glow,
Chairs and wordsearches ran to my feet,
And the ceiling fell on my head.

Everything started shaking, even my feet didn't stand this,
I felt my hand touch the crumbled ceiling,
And my body swinging from left to right,
Then, out of the window I flew!

In a bush I landed, prickles on my back,
And now they call me 'Superboy',
And I have to travel in a pack.

I don't know what it was,
Maybe it was too much friction,
Maybe it *was* me!
But all I can tell is something,
    something,
        something,
           I forgot!

Selin Ozkosar (10)
Merlin Primary School, Bromley

Football

F ootball is the best
O n the pitch the football players go wild
O n and off the players go
T he team score a goal
B ounce, bounce the football goes
A rsenal are the best team in the world
L osers cry
L inesmen are sometimes dodgy!

Kieran Hopkins (10)
Merlin Primary School, Bromley

Friendship

(Dedicated to my best friend Lois)

Along in the playground
I was playing with my friend,
I said to her our friendship would never end,
We will play together now or never,
We will play together forever and ever.
Friendship is something that you should never throw away,
Friendship is something you should keep every day,
Because you may need it some day,
I did!

Sammie Delany (11)
Merlin Primary School, Bromley

Lightning

A fire starter
A tree killer
A life destroyer
A building burner
A forest lighter
A body trembler.

Luke O'Toole
Merlin Primary School, Bromley

Tigers

T iny claws,
I tchy paws,
G etting bored,
E veryone snored,
R unning around,
S afe and sound.

Adem Hassan (10)
Merlin Primary School, Bromley

Ways Of The Wind

As the wind ran right past my face,
It danced and pranced past my face,
As the wind ran right past my face,
It leapt and crept past my face.

I will chase that wind far and near,
Its sound whistling in my ear.

As I chased after the wind,
I danced and pranced after the wind,
As I chased after the wind,
I leapt and crept after the wind.

I will chase that wind far and near,
Its sound whistling through my ear.

As the wind ran right away from me,
It danced and pranced right away from me,
As the wind ran right away from me,
It leapt and crept away from me,
And it finally got away from me.

Joe Taylor (10)
Merton Court School, Sidcup

Winter

W hy my favourite time of the year
 I s playing in the snow
N ever really wanting it to go
T ogether we have so much fun
E verybody trying to snowball everyone
R emember what it was once like, come back snow tonight.

Joshua White (10)
Merton Court School, Sidcup

Holiday

Sitting on the aeroplane
My family and me
Looking out the window
At the beautiful blue sea.

The plane starts moving downwards
It was time for us to land
Everybody rushes to the front
They can't wait to see the sand.

We get our cases from the airport
And arrive at our hotel
The sun is shining brightly
It will be lovely, I can tell.

My parents take us to our room
Mum unpacks, that is the rule
Because me, Dad and my sister
Will be swimming in the pool.

Blue sky and lots of sunshine
Yellow beaches and calm sea
Coconuts and palm trees
This is the holiday for me.

Sam Lateo (10)
Merton Court School, Sidcup

Roaming Free

Roaming free is how a lion spends his day,
The thing to do now is to catch his prey,
Creeping stealthily, stalking in silence,
Getting ready to strike out in violence.

He catches his food with a pounce and a bite,
After he has won a challenging fight.
He has not eaten for long days on end,
Now with the vultures he has to contend.

Upon the trunk of a tree he paddles his long, sharp claws,
Gritting his pointy teeth and washing his furry paws.
The winnowing wind blows his matted mane around,
Now by the disturbing hyenas he has been found.

Rapidly jumping up, his smooth fur on end,
Hyenas, that are impossible to befriend.
With a sharp sprint followed by a fierce roar,
He scares them away and returns for more.

Bethan Warman (10)
Merton Court School, Sidcup

The Toy Soldier

When you are sleeping,
The toy soldier is not,
When you are in bed,
He stands guarded.

He stands very tall,
And he always looks smart,
With a button-down jacket
And shiny black shoes.

He's always on track,
He never lets things slip,
He's always armed,
With a gun on his shoulder.

Ellis Rose Crawshaw (10)
Merton Court School, Sidcup

The Lion

The lion, the king of the jungle,
The top killer in the African savannah,
He has the eyes of an eagle,
He has the speed of a cheetah,
And the strength of a bear.

He spots his prey, watches it,
He never takes his eyes off it,
He gets up, walks to it cautiously,
He blends in with his surroundings,
He will wait and wait for the right moment.

Then suddenly, he jumps out of the grass,
He runs and runs his opponent to the ground,
It is the right moment, he leaps onto his prey,
Brings it to the ground,
And in a few seconds it is dead.

He calls over the rest of the pride,
So they can all get a piece of flesh,
Devouring all the meat they can gorge into their mouths,
Then they leave it to scavengers.

Sam Griffin-Beat (11)
Merton Court School, Sidcup

The Abandoned Dog

Abandoned,
Forlorn,
Solitary,
And isolated.
I sit there all alone,
No one around me,
No one to care and love me,
Everybody's left me and dumped me
In an old wooden box.
My lead that is tied to the box
Is pulling me down like manacles.
The boring trees are all I have to look at.
The box is closing me in
It's making me feel claustrophobic,
The best thing I can see is the dark night
With twinkling stars.
I am alone,
All alone.

Charlee Brace-Bywater (10)
Merton Court School, Sidcup

Butterfly

How I adore the butterfly,
Fluently, gracefully it flutters by,
Spreading its bright, fragile wings,
Looking the most beautiful of all things.

Born short, ugly and eats and eats,
Not knowing any of its future feats,
Eventually daring to venture out,
No longer looking ungraceful and stout.

Escaping, soaring high,
Ascending into the summer sky,
Roaming, free,
Exploring what it has yet to see.

Katerina Charalambous (11)
Merton Court School, Sidcup

Under The Fantastic Ocean

Under the fantastic ocean,
You will be able to find,
Fish like rainbows,
And fish that are dull.

The rocky pieces of coral,
Look like a coloured forest,
Candyfloss pink, blood-red,
And in variety of shapes.

The seaweed in the ocean,
Is like wavy hair,
It can be grass green,
Or black as coal.

Tiny anchovies swim around,
As well as enormous tuna,
Fish that can puff themselves up,
And fish that look like horses.

There are sharks that are fierce,
Like a great white,
Or sharks that are weird,
Like a hammerhead.

The world's largest mammals,
Are beneath the waves,
Like the killer whale eating fish,
Or humpback whale swallowing plankton.

Underneath the ocean,
Is a wonderful place to be,
It is beautiful and quiet,
There is so much more to see.

Andrew Clode (10)
Merton Court School, Sidcup

Riding Through The Snow

As I sat there in that tank, I looked up and saw our flag flapping
with white spots all over it.
The hammer and sickle glint in the pale light and as they do so,
snow falls through the hatch.
As I stand up I see a sea of white snow blanketing the ground
and outlines of ruined buildings smouldering.
Then I look to the side and see my comrades pursuing close behind.
Sun is covered by clouds determined to discourage us; I look back
and see a flag being swept away in the wind,
Then I see something that chills me to the marrow.
I hear the cries of people shouting, 'Germans!' They are right.
German tanks thunder in the distance, small puffs of smoke emerge
from the shadows and the roaring screech is not far behind.
A massive bang and I am sent into shellshock.
More explosions follow.
I smell evil coming from the enemy; the scent of rotten eggs
is in the air.
I smell lead coming from the rounds one by one being loaded
and sent into the fiery jaws of Hell.
We receive a blow and lead is splattered into my face; some goes
into my mouth - it tastes like a scorching powder and as I rub
my tongue over it, it pierces my mouth.
Instinctively, I grab a handful of snow and stuff between
my burning lips, its ice-cold features are a relief.
As I pick up a round it feels smooth until I reach the ridge in it,
I quickly load it in and it fires.
We are hit again and I grab hold of something.
This time it feels tough and I notice it is the jacket of one of
my comrades, or should I say former comrades.
Finally we halt and through the swirling smog notice that all
the German tanks are ablaze.

Michael Currans (11)
Merton Court School, Sidcup

At The Seaside

At the seaside I can see;
The gentle waves crashing towards the beach,
Seagulls overhead circling the sky round and round,
People swimming in the deep blue sea,
Adults sunbathing on the carpet of sand,
And the children making sandcastles with their spades and buckets.

At the seaside I can hear;
The sound of the seagulls,
The waves roaring,
People chatting,
And children laughing as they enjoy the joy.

At the seaside I can feel;
The sand sticking to my feet,
The cold water of the sea,
The hard surface of the shiny pebbles,
The ice cream as it melts in my mouth,
And the intense heat beating against my skin making me sweat.

At the seaside I can taste;
The salty taste of the sea water,
The tasteful flavour of the ice cream,
Dripping from the cone,
And the mouth-watering fizzy drinks bubbling inside my mouth.

Vincent Lam (10)
Merton Court School, Sidcup

Why I Don't Have My Homework?

My dog ate my homework,
I really don't know why,
He already had his dinner,
I really did try.

What will you say next,
You naughty little child,
I don't know what to do with you,
You're always in trouble.

My brother ripped my homework,
He threw it in the bin,
I think I made him angry,
I really didn't win.

What is going on,
You naughty little child,
I have no idea what to do with you,
You're always in trouble.

I didn't do my homework, Miss,
I didn't want to do it,
I would like to be expelled,
I'd like to stay away, I'll kick and hit.

Well if you want to be expelled,
You naughty little child,
Your dog and brother did nothing,
It was you, you, you.

Alyssa Matharu (11)
Merton Court School, Sidcup

The Meadow

To lay in a meadow, what a wondrous thing
Listening to the bees buzzing, birds singing
Grasshoppers hopping among the blades of grass
Oh, how I love this tranquil meadow.

Children running and playing in the park
Cows grazing with their young in the distance
People riding their horses, galloping with joy
Oh, how I love the majestic meadow

Families enjoying the day, having a picnic
To smell the sweet smell of freshly baked cakes
All the sounds and sights of a beautiful day
Oh, how I love the fabulous meadow

The sky is sparkling blue all the way to Heaven
Only a few wispy clouds floating high above
The sun shining so bright it hurts your eyes
Oh, how I love the shimmering meadow

As the sun gently sinks into the horizon
Shadows creep slowly across the grass floor
The day is ending and sadly it's time to go
Oh, how I've loved my day in the meadow.

Jamie-Leigh O'Reilly (10)
Merton Court School, Sidcup

Robin Redbreast

Robin redbreast so tender in flight
Robin redbreast so colourful and bright
Robin redbreast you are the best
Oh how sweet you are, robin redbreast
Robin redbreast
The most beautiful creature in the world

Sweet robin redbreast, so fragile and mild
Oh robin redbreast as sweet as a young child
Robin redbreast
The most beautiful creature in the world

Robin redbreast, perched silent and still
Sweet robin redbreast as fragile as a daffodil
Robin redbreast
The most beautiful creature in the world

Robin redbreast, your feathers so neat
Robin redbreast sing your merry tune, tweet, tweet
Robin redbreast
The most beautiful creature in the world

Robin redbreast so tender in flight
Robin redbreast so colourful and bright
Robin redbreast you are the best
Oh how sweet you are robin redbreast
Robin redbreast
The most beautiful creature in the world.

Henry Pyle (10)
Merton Court School, Sidcup

The Playground

I can hear children chattering amongst themselves,
Laughing and screaming as well,
Children playing football and 'it',
Running after each other, keeping fit.

The football feels hard and round,
The playground fence feels cold and strong,
Excitement fills the playground,
As children play, skip and run along.

Trees, shrubs surrounds us,
As birds fly and sing above,
Benches covered with sitting children who don't rush,
Waiting for the whistle's sound.

I can taste the moisture in the air,
And the cool breeze along my cheeks,
As I rush, sprint and call out a dare,
I at last reach and touch my friends.

I can smell the freshness in the air,
The fragrance of the flowerbeds,
Honeysuckle, roses and freshly cut grass,
In the nearby field.

The whistle blows to quieten us down,
We all stand still like stone,
Then children gather up in lines,
To slowly return to their classes.

Harpiar Seehra (10)
Merton Court School, Sidcup

My Baby Brother

For months I waited,
Anxious to see,
Wondering and dreaming
Of how he would be.

The day he was born
Was special to all our family,
Perfect and healthy,
A baby brother for me.

His eyes, nose and ears
Were the cutest I have seen,
Lying here peacefully
Just like a dream.

He began to smile,
And made little sounds,
Growing bigger and bigger,
Looking at all that was around.

Now he knows me,
He screams with glee,
Jumping with excitement,
Just to see me.

What will he be like?
I just do not know,
But my baby brother
Just continues to grow.

Sophie Taylor-Jones (10)
Merton Court School, Sidcup

The Deep, Dark Wood

As I crept cautiously over the fence
Into the deep, dark wood,
The trees were continuously whispering to one another.
A blanket of mist covered the wood
While some rested on my tongue.
The darkness is enclosed around me,
Leaves are rustling, twigs are breaking,
Creatures howling loudly,
Though I was not afraid, my shadow was comforting me.
A magical light came down
As the moon shone like sequins.
Suddenly there was a sound coming from a bush,
Strange, thrilling and frightening.
All at the same time
Something was running at such an unimaginable pace
Which painted me with a coat of mystery and awe.
I then turned to leave saying,
'Goodbye,'
To the whispering trees.
Then I went home,
My shadow and I.

I knew I would
Never forget
This night.

Lauren Thomas (11)
Merton Court School, Sidcup

Flight Of The Dove

Soaring through the air,
Gracefully gliding over glistening lakes,
Swooping down into the trees,
Swiftly rising again,

Bringing love, peace and hope,

Soft is the feather,
Coat pure white as snow,

The dove flies overhead,
Spreading its light over the land,
Making the world green once more,
Flower and trees cover the earth,

Bringing love, peace and hope,

Dipping into the valleys,
Diving over mountain peaks,
Dodging through the forest trees,
Speeding over windy moors,

Bringing love, peace and hope,

Finally coming to rest on the ark,
Bringing the olive branch,
A symbol of
Love, peace and hope.

Edward Wallis (10)
Merton Court School, Sidcup

A Waterfall

A stream
Starts its journey
At the top
Gliding down
The mountainside
Drifting peacefully
Down
Until there is a
Roar!
And the mountain
Loses its floor
There is a rush
And a splash
Like a savage
Monster
Then it is peaceful
Again
Until the next
Drop!

Joseph Ives (10)
Merton Court School, Sidcup

Football

F ootball is the greatest sport,
O ff to the park I go,
O ver to the football pitch,
T owards the open goal,
B elt it in the top hand corner,
A ah, what a perfect goal,
L aughter overcomes me,
L et's have another go!

Joseph Ansell (10)
Merton Court School, Sidcup

Can You Guess Who I Am?

I'm blue, shiny and silky,
I love it when people come up and touch me,
When people feed me from their hands.

I think it's great to take people out on my back,
When they tickle me under the chin,
When they stroke my nose.

It's great to explore the deep blue sea,
It's cold and refreshing when the waves hit my face,
When the gentle breeze reaches me.

I love it when I dive to the bottom of the sea,
When I find new things I've never seen before,
When I reach a cave I've never seen before.

Yasmin Mustafa (11)
Merton Court School, Sidcup

Guess Which Insect This Is . . .

Venomous killer,
Busy worker,
Venom injector,
Fast web spinner,
Eight-legged frightener,
A two-fanged devil,
An eight-legged freak,
A furry insect eater,
Has art on its back,
By now I hope that you have guessed
What insect this is
Because this is what I am –
A spider!

Imtiyaz Zaman (10)
Monega Primary School, London

My Family

My mum is sad,
She drives me absolutely mad.
My mum thinks my dad is lazy,
But my dad thinks my mum is crazy.

My sister likes to have fun,
She often likes to bathe in the sun.
My brother likes to make a racket,
Especially when eating crisps from a packet.

My aunt thinks she's really funny,
When she is dressed up as a bunny.
My uncle likes to have a snooze,
After he's had a lot of booze.

My gran is the best,
But she can be a right pest.
My granny also loves to nag,
Especially when Grandad's having a fag.

My cousins are such a pain,
They could drive you insane.
They are always making a noise,
When they are talking about boys.

Now all that's left to talk about is me,
In this poem about my family.
When I grow up I want to be an author,
And be driven by a chauffeur!

How better can I describe my family?
I love them so dearly.
They are just a bunch of ordinary people,
I wouldn't change them for the world
Cos that's my family!

Aysha Patel (10)
Monega Primary School, London

Joy

Joy is yellow like the blazing hot sun,
Pink like the children laughing with lots of fun.

Joy sounds like birds chirping,
The cold breeze blowing.

Joy tastes like a sweet bun,
Very hot straight from the oven.

Joy smells like pretty flowers,
Scent from the bees buzzing around for hours.

Joy looks like children playing in the park,
Flowers blooming and bees buzzing.

Joy feels like a bright fluorescent sunflower blowing at you,
A tulip kissing you too.

Pooja Samji (10)
Monega Primary School, London

Classroom Rules

Rules, rules, what are rules?
They are simple guidelines for the class to follow and use.

No talking when the teacher is or you won't know what to do,
Not only that you'll get it wrong and you'll get in trouble too.

When answering a question put your hand up in the air,
Shouting out is very wrong and totally unfair.

When you get some homework complete it nice and neat,
If required get your parents to help but make sure you don't cheat.

Do what the teacher tells you and you'll have a happy day,
Follow these simple rules and you'll get a good grade A.

Sachin Dabasia (11)
Monega Primary School, London

Loneliness

Always told to go away,
Never asked to come and join in,
Being called names and made fun of,
Never good comments or good things.

Even in a crowd still alone,
Wherever I look no one's there,
Like everyone's gone far, far away,
Disappeared into thin air.

The feeling is dreadful,
And appallingly deep,
That every depressing night,
I cry myself to sleep.

Now everyone's gone away,
So they still cannot see,
That they made something feel rejected,
And that something is *me!*

Johura Khatun (11)
Monega Primary School, London

Leaves

I sway in the breeze,
And scatter about,
I'm there when you need me,
To shuffle and crunch.

I can be all different colours,
Red, orange, yellow and green,
I grow in the spring,
And fall in the autumn.

Sonyea Uddin (11)
Monega Primary School, London

My Favourite Seasons

This is my poem, it's about seasons in your lives,
If you can guess what season is which, give me a five.

This is my favourite,
Cool, breezy weather,
Beautiful flowers spring from their buds,
They are as fragrant as ever,
Gusts of wind, showers of rain,
This season is on the wane.

This is my favourite,
You can hop,
Playing in the park,
Eating lollipops,
It might get sunny,
Bees making honey.

This is my favourite,
Use your mind,
You can get fall,
How many leaves can you find?
It might get a bit chilly outside,
So stay inside.

This is my real, real favourite,
Some people do not like it snowing,
But some people love it,
When it is blowing,
The Christmas spirits,
Looking outside for shocking lightning.

Could you guess?
Hope you do,
Does not matter,
If you lose.

Kaisha Mandalia (10)
Monega Primary School, London

Rules Rap

If you don't listen to the rules,
You are a fool.
If you talk when the teacher is talking,
To the head teacher you will be walking.
If you are bad,
The teacher will go mad.
If you don't walk on the left side of the stairs,
Get ready to meet your worst nightmares.
From the top of your head,
To the tip of your toes,
Your tears will be dropping for your worst day woes.
If you push in the line for your lunch from others,
At the end of the day you will be crying in front of your mothers.
If you are going with your mates to play chicken,
You are going to remember the story of 'Chicken Licken'.
So what should I say at the end of the day,
Stay away from the lorries, be safe, not sorry.

Anzal Javaid (11)
Monega Primary School, London

Anger

Anger is a very fiery orange colour like the sun.
Anger sounds like whizzing fireworks.
Anger tastes like your mouth is very dry.
Anger smells like dry bark.
Anger looks like everything is flashing red, orange, brown and yellow.
Anger feels like an earthquake going on inside your body.
Anger reminds me of my mum shouting *loud!*

Sachin Patel (10)
Monega Primary School, London

What Is This World?

What is this world?
Somewhere there is land without use
Somewhere there are people fighting for land.

What is this world?
Somewhere people are risking their lives
Somewhere people are scared of death.

What is this world?
Somewhere people are thirsty for a sip of water
Somewhere there is countless water without any use.

What is this world?
Somewhere people are rich
Somewhere people are living in poverty.

What is this world?
Somewhere there is happiness and new birth
Somewhere there is sorrow and people dying.

Rimsha Iqbal (10)
Monega Primary School, London

Year 5000

Dogs go around on rollerskates
Cats go to the gym with their mates
Fishmongers sell sharks and whales
They also have kick powered scales
PS50s are 50p
Animals have automatic feed
Dragons jump and shout
Robots spend 24 hours out
Yet people still fall in love
Like a pair of turtle doves.

Harris Rehman (11)
Monega Primary School, London

Fruit And Veg Fun

Watermelon's nice and juicy,
It tastes very, very sweet,
And makes your mouth water,
Some people love watermelon,
Do you?

Carrots are so crunchy,
Oranges have a tender softness to them,
Lettuces have a crunchy feel,
Lychees are so juicy,
I love fruit,
All I want to do is eat it.

Now do you like eating fruit?
Well I certainly do.
Strawberries are bright red and juicy,
And raspberries are too.

Sunita Luggah (10)
Monega Primary School, London

The Snail

One slimy thing
Sitting on some mud,
Slithers up a fence
With a shelter on its back.
Never too fast,
Never too slow,
It always hates salt,
Can you guess what it is?

Fariha Rahman (11)
Monega Primary School, London

Families

Oh, we all have families from top to toe,
It really doesn't matter if we fight or grow.
We may bicker, we may squabble day to day,
But who knows if we'll quarrel when world war comes to stay.

Each family has a comedian,
Who laughs from morning till dusk,
Plays jokes and pranks without a sound,
And nobody knows they're around.

Families contain a computer whizz,
Knows all the tricks in the book,
Sits day and night on the computer seat,
With a slice of bread and meat.

We all have an artist who draws super stylish,
From clothes to models which is the definite nicest,
Papier maché is one of a favourite,
Skilful and talented you think you're the greatest.

The cook is the best with delicious food,
Great tasting cuisines with a lot for you too,
Usually Mum, but Dad won't mind,
Wearing an apron, how excitingly divine.

We've come to the end,
And although you won't believe it,
We all love each other though we may still hit,
You call your sisters gorillas and brothers Frankenstein,
Though possibly true, still keep in mind,
You have secret feelings and so do I.

Humna Iqbal (9)
Monega Primary School, London

India

When I wake up every morning.
I remember the sun in India rising,
It was a mellow yellow colour,
And was like no other.
I remember the moon sparkling,
And the stars around were glittering.
I remember the food that we had in the evening,
Spicy curries, rice and sweet things.
I remember going to the sea,
Picking flowers in the garden,
And chasing bees.
I remember my nanny's lap where I would sleep -
I would have lovely dreams.

Mamta Vaiyata (10)
Monega Primary School, London

Blue Marlin

B ulleting, lancing through the coral reef
L ike the graceful sailfish
U ndertaking the fishing hook
E ntire ocean is its territory.

M etallic blue scales shimmering and shining in the sunlight
A thletic and streamlined
R ocketing past the sailfish
L ashing the water with its tail
I ncredible speed
N othing stops it!

Huon Vassie (9)
Oval Primary School, Croydon

The Jungle

The powerful lion, the great maned cat,
Is even more cunning than a rat.
The tiger's stripes flash danger,
To any animal that seems a stranger.
The giraffe is taller than a tree,
One of the tallest animals to be.
The elephant's trunk is grey and long,
Its body is huge and its feet are strong.
The cheetah is amazingly fast,
If you blink you'll miss it go past.
The snake slithers as it shall pass,
As it moves it hides in the grass.
In a tree the parrot will squawk
And on the ground it will walk.
The falcon rules the sky,
To go near it will be a big try.
The vulture is a bald predator,
And it has a very sharp claw.
The jungle is wild, the jungle is free,
The jungle is a danger to you and me!

Paul Anderson (9)
Oval Primary School, Croydon

Seals

S lippery like ice
E ats fish a lot
A nose black and shiny
L oves to swim
S eals are my favourite animal.

Matthew Anderson (8)
Oval Primary School, Croydon

My Magical Adventure

As I dive down to a new world,
I see dolphins dancing
And diving up and down
All over the sea,
Diving on a bit further
And I see a shipwreck,
Like a clump of coral,
There's an octopus on a treasure chest,
A coating of barnacles
Encrust the shipwreck.

I find the key to the treasure chest,
Edging forwards I scare the octopus,
I open the chest and find gold and diamonds.
I am surprised, I never thought
I would find treasure where I am,
As I am in the Bahamas.
I have finished my adventure
As I swim back to the normal world.

Hannah Edmundson (9)
St Joseph's Convent School, London

The Underwater World

Jolly jellyfish, its head made of jelly
Sly shark swoops into action
Crabs scuttle in the sand in a swoosh
Seaweed swiftly sweeps in the swaying of the breeze

Colourful clownfish coolly clown
Stingrays trying to sting me
I dodge them like I'm on the dodgems
Piranhas staring like I'm their lunch

I swim to the beach
For the last time I look back
I see the dolphins dive
I see the fish flip and an oily oyster looks at me.

Grace McAuliffe (9)
St Joseph's Convent School, London

Panic

Seaweed tickles my leg
'Beware of the crab!'
Whirling, twirling mermaids
Mischievous as monkeys

Angelfish with halos
I bet they play the harp
As angelic as could ever be

Mermaids, mermaids
Millions of mermaids
Tails as green as emeralds
Flaxen curls and teeth like pearls
Magical mermaids muttering

Look, what's that?
100 teeth, deadly eyes, gills
Sly and slick
Fast and quick
It's a killer

A seaweed plant grabs my leg
I need to run higher and higher
I'm losing oxygen.
Crunch!

He takes a bite for my oxygen tank,
I'm nearly at the top
I start at front crawl
Then go onto back.

'Mum! Mum!
There's a shark!'

'Oh no!'

Annabelle Juffs (9)
St Joseph's Convent School, London

My Underwater Poem

As I dive through the crystal clear water
Bubbles bursting like crystal balls
Showing me the future.

Mermaids swimming with fishes
Mermaids' hair floating
Through the waving seaweed.

Peacefully I swam in the great blue
Suddenly a hollow comes to view
A shipwreck, a treasure chest.

Jellyfish swim past me
I must be careful so they won't sting me
It's silent, it's clear, it's just how I imagined it.

I swim back up to take my tea
And I wonder if I could dig deeper
Next time.

Tanyia Ahmed (9)
St Joseph's Convent School, London

The Black Pearl's Curse

As I see the light of the sea
I dig down deep to find my quest
Maybe I'll see a jellyfish
With the black pearl's curse.

I see a pearl, it dazzles my eyes
I feel like I'm floating in the skies
I turn and twist and see my fist
Touching a box of gold
It's magic, it's magic, it's so fantastic
I feel that I'm full of joy and ecstatic.

I go down deeper and
As I find the wrecks of
History
I go in to explore.

Julide Ayger (9)
St Joseph's Convent School, London

Jessica's Jolly, Jelly Jellyfish

Under the sea,
I can see,
Iridescent shimmering
A jolly purple jellyfish.

It floats below me,
As low as it can go,
Out of the blue a sea horse strays,
Slowly swooping down low.

Never-ending seaweed waves up high,
The stray sea horse swoops from side to side,
The chromatic jellyfish
Goes to catch the tide.

As I swam back to the beach
The breathtaking fishes,
Were out of my reach.

Jessica Anthony (9)
St Joseph's Convent School, London

Swimming In The Deep

I dive into the perfect blue water,
Scared at first but then notice
The beautiful secrets of the deep.
I touch a bush with my finger
It then disappears in a playful puff of smoke.

Swimming away from the mysterious exploding bush
I see a beautiful angelfish
Breathtaking as it led me to a moulded wreck,
A golden box inside I hoped.

Suddenly a pain surged through my body
I'd been stung by a jellyfish!
I swam back to the shore leaving my flaxen-curled mermaids,
Wary of sharks and delicate dolphins all behind.

Philippa Archibald (10)
St Joseph's Convent School, London

The Cold, Deep, Blue Sea

Bubbles like pearls
Bubbles, bubbles.
Beware of the bubbles that sting.
Gold that sparkles,
Dazzling my eyes,
My eyes are pearls.

The sting of jellyfish
Hurts my hand!
Bits of sting in my hand
I pick them out
To make it all better.

The slime of an octopus
Makes me shiver.
The cold, cold water,
As I go down
I see barnacles and fish
Oh I wish I was an oyster
So I could live there.

I am filled with joy,
I have found a box of gold,
Going down deeper
I find sharks
Covering a wreck with coins
That is wonderful!

Annabeth Ravensdale (9)
St Joseph's Convent School, London

The Deep Blue Sea

I swim in the sapphire sea
Not knowing what to expect.
I dive into another world
The creatures feel like birds in the sky
As they pass by.

All the creatures glide
With eyes like crystal
In the peaceful water,
Trickling like small bubbles
The oily oyster sweeps a pearl.
A sea horse swishes through the water,
An emerald colour sparks a light.

I see a colour, strange grey
It spells trouble,
A sly shark sweeps and spies,
All the creatures hide or die.
After a while it goes away
All the creatures come out again.

Loanna Katana (9)
St Joseph's Convent School, London

Mysterious Things Under The Sea

As I go in the sea
I see mysteries - things like jellyfish and sea turtles
A sea turtle is walking as slowly as possible in the sand
A diver comes diving in as quickly as possible
All the jellyfish have swum away from me
I go deep down and I find a dolphin as blue as the sea
I look left and right and I find a shipwreck that has barnacles all over it
In the distance I see a shark
Its sharp teeth shining in the water
Panicking I swim up to the boat, the shark goes past me!
I see a peach-coloured jellyfish going home
And I think I should go home too.

Joanna Mall (9)
St Joseph's Convent School, London

Under The Water

Under the water,
The seaweed is waving all around,
Covering up the treasure box,
Lonely and brown.

Crunchy crabs come around,
Below me and on the ground,
An oyster shows me its pearl,
I go to catch it, then it curls.

I see a daring dolphin,
Swimming as nice as can be,
A shark behind it,
Finding its tea.

Panicking I swim back to the shore,
Up, up, up I go wandering the wonders
Under the sea.

Nicole Ashraf (10)
St Joseph's Convent School, London

Under The Sea

Delicate dolphins dive and dash
Swordfish noses make a flash
Under the deep blue sea
Magical sights waiting for me.

Angelic angelfish are the angels of the ocean
Seaweed swaying in very slow motion
Jumpy jellyfish jump and journey
Sticky barnacles are very curly.

I see a treasure chest - gold and sparkly
I try to open it, it will not budge
Oh no! my oxygen is running out!
Panicking I swim to the surface
Back to the noisy crowd.

Lily Atherton (10)
St Joseph's Convent School, London

Down In The Deep

Dolphins jumping in the air,
Like little feathers above the air,
You see a golden chest with a golden coin inside.
Frantic flippers flapping away into the distance.

Seaweed swaying and swooshing
Like thick pieces of string,
I say, a little crab which runs away,
Is a shark coming?

Crunchy crabs that crawl away
Are getting scared in every way,
Just a little help
Would be the way.

What's scaring them?
Is it a shark snapping its teeth at them,
Trying to get its dinner?

Fast fish flash by
Like a little crash,
I tried and swam to get them back.

As I swim back to the shore
I wonder if . . .

Louise Bradbury (10)
St Joseph's Convent School, London

My Underwater Poem

Gleeful leaping dolphins
Bounce up and down
Swishing seaweed tickles my feet
Pearls like silvery moonlight
Pop in my hand!
I see them in crystal clear water.

Magic mermaids swim
By my side -
A box of treasure
To my surprise!

A silent sea horse
Makes the letter 's'
Sly sharks
Are sinister
With eyes like rubies.

A stroke of shivers
Goes down my spine.
I swim to the shore
What an adventure I've had!

Kate Roberts (9)
St Joseph's Convent School, London

What's Under The Sea?

As I dive down under the sea
My feet are trapped in seaweed
I struggle out of the green fishing net
As I pass the fishes happily swimming
I find a treasure chest buried.

I pick up the treasure chest
Until I feel something pinching me . . .
It is an orange crab
Snapping at my swimming suit!

I am happy in the clear water
The colour is like crystal skies.
I see something pink in the emerald seaweed
It stings like a bee
It's a jellyfish!

I float away from that stinging fish.
In the far distance I see an electric eel,
Swimming away to my land.
I will never forget this day.

Trisha Seeromben (9)
St Joseph's Convent School, London

Underwater Land

Going to the underwater land I spy
Underwater leaves as seaweed sways like weeds

Look! A treasure chest waiting to be opened
See the golden coins spread out in my hand!

There a ray of sunlight shows me that it was shells
So as I flip-flap, flip-flop flippers
Flappering around I swim away

Terimelda Kyomuhendo (9)
St Joseph's Convent School, London

The Deep Blue Sea

I dive down into the deep,
The water sends a shiver down my spine,
This peaceful place so different to the normal world.
My breath is taken away,
Landing on the seabed,
I see the crystal clear water glistening in the sun,
Rainbow-coloured fish swim by.
The lime-green seaweed swishes from side to side,
Little fishes swiftly dart through the maze of seaweed at my feet,
Which tickles my senses as I swim past it.
Crawling crabs scatter in all directions,
Following one I drift onto an old wreck,
Sitting lost in time in the deep blue.
Beside it lies a hollow with silver coins and a treasure chest,
Many bars of gold,
Sparkling, twinkling bars of gold.
I have to leave the sea behind
As I run out of oxygen,
But I will come back another day,
To find what lies in the deep blue sea.

Emma Flynn (10)
St Joseph's Convent School, London

Under The Deep Blue Sea

Under the deep blue sea,
As wide as a mountain range,
As deep as the sky,
The brightly coloured fishes,
Awaiting me to come swimming by.

Jumping jellyfish jog for joy,
I see an oyster,
A silvery moonlit pearl.

Silky sea horses swim safely,
Crafty crabs crease their claws.
Shiny seaweed swaying softly,
Frantic fish flying away.

The silky dolphins come swimming past,
Trying to talk as they swim.
I swim up to my land,
Saying farewell to all my ocean friends.

Emily Wong (9)
St Joseph's Convent School, London

The Dark, Deep Blue Sea

As I enter the dark, deep blue sea,
A fantastic tropical fish
Swims past me.

I see lots of crawling crabs on the floor,
Then later on comes quite a lot more.

As I look into the distance I could see
A very old ship,
Then a shoal of fish came along.

I see a box of treasure to my surprise
And then comes a mermaid,
That sits by my side!

Sea horses race by our sides
In an ocean gymkhana
Where my favourite horse wins.

Claudia Holmes (10)
St Joseph's Convent School, London

My Underwater World

I dive down into the sea
What a beautiful world
A school of jellyfish swim by me
Jumping jellyfish in the sea

A shipwreck dumped in the sand
Glowing gold in the middle of my hand
It's peaceful down in the sea
Lovely and restful

Dolphins dashing in the deep blue sea
I watch them dash by me
Leaving splashes everywhere
I watch in slow motion

I love the ocean
I had a magical time
With all the colourful fish,
And even a wreck
Dumped in the sand,
I cannot wait to return.

Olivia Collins (9)
St Joseph's Convent School, London

The Magical Sea

The five peaceful fish swim through the air of the water,
A magical mermaid bubbles in the water,
The mysterious treasure chest moves
Like a breathing pearl,
Slippery seaweed sways
Swiftly in the sea.

The windy sand gets into my eyes,
Like a flannel on my face,
I see a green emerald
Near the windy sand,
But wait!

Then I see the mysterious treasure chest again
The creatures swim quickly like a racing car
I hear a voice above it
Then I realise it's my mum
Calling me for tea.

Thandiwe Adeshiyan (9)
St Joseph's Convent School, London

A New World

Under the sea
Where creatures swim
I watch them passing by
Big ones, small ones
Some with ripped fins.

Green swaying coral
With seaweed
Right beside it
Mermaids swishing
Through the clear water
With beautiful hair
Shiny as gold.

Starfish as yellow as the sun
Crabs with claws that crunch
At the bottom of the sea
A rusty old treasure chest
In the chest are jewels as
Colourful as the rainbow.

Lucinda Dawson (10)
St Joseph's Convent School, London

The Wind

The wind comes from a lightning-sharp Formula 1 car
Driven by Michael Schumacher in his top class vehicle
Going at the record speed.
The wind is a vicious greyhound, going at a fast speed in the wild.
At night, the greyhound howls towards the moon,
Sending shivers down your spine,
Giving you the spooks while you're sleeping.
Going so fast, hunting for its prey, it sprints in hunger.

Courtney Francis (10)
St Luke's Primary School, London

Volcano

A volcano is an enraged phoenix,
Fiery and red.
He demolishes houses, farms and sheds,
With his deadly talons and hazardous beak.

Lava meteors into every space on Earth
Boulders tumbling down the volcano in a
Rapid pace,
Crashing into precious things and wasting land,
Even burning the beach's sand.

But then, it stops so sudden, suddenly
Drops into the sea,
Fades away and the phoenix flees
He flies back to the volcano to start all over again.

Bipul Deb (11)
St Luke's Primary School, London

Avalanche

An avalanche is a crazy ape
Crushing everything in its path
With mighty power in its hands
Hurdling over the trees
Leaving destruction and chaos behind it
While screaming at people
Getting in a temper easily
Trapping people in the nearest place.

Jonathan Bradford (11)
St Luke's Primary School, London

Lightning

Lightning is a fast cheetah
Runs faster than 200 miles per hour
They're the only speedy creatures
That's because they've more power.

They're simply rapid
Exceedingly smart
Truly quick
Nippy as a dart.

Lightning is a rapid *flash!*
It makes some people glare at it
It definitely has a colour
Extremely, exceedingly brilliant
But it flashes for a bit.

Lightning is electricity
A torch shining from
Heaven!

Zack Karhani (11)
St Luke's Primary School, London

Volcano

A volcano is an erupting dragon
That is too fast, too furious.

That is an angry volcano
And it gets so fierce and roars, roars, to kill.

That dragon's fire is faster than lightning
It erupts in a storm
Exploding fireballs up into the breezy sky.

Burak Gunduz (11)
St Luke's Primary School, London

The Meteor

A meteor is a dragon's fireball
Blown furiously on Earth
Burning through the Earth's atmosphere
With his pointy teeth and slimy tongue
He breathes a fireball
Slowly, slowly burns in
Eating away
Into the depths of the Earth.

He breathes a fireball so quick
That a shock of chaos begins
The people run wild
But they have nowhere to go.

Sometimes he plays
Makes the meteor go round and round
The Earth's atmosphere
And strikes.

Shuhala Ahad (11)
St Luke's Primary School, London

Volcano

A volcano is a vicious T-rex
Furious at his prey
Camouflaged in the cave
Waiting for his prey
One step away
Licking his watery lips
Crunch!
Ripping the fresh skin off his victim
Scaring dinosaurs
Scratch! Three bloody scratches.

Harry Edwards (10)
St Luke's Primary School, London

Volcano

A volcano is a fearsome dragon
Swelling and scaly
With his vicious rumbling and tumbling lava
Flying through the air
Waiting and waiting to appear
When the fearless dragon strikes
He burns everything that steps up to him
Whenever it's dark or dim he is bound to attack.
Daytime the dragon rests
Fear no harm, you should be fine
Just stay well away from the volcano.

Tyrus Williams (11)
St Luke's Primary School, London

Hurricane

A hurricane is a sprinting cheetah
Running in circles
Looking for things to grab
Destroying everything it sees
And pretending to calm down
But really getting ready to pounce.

It growls, slowly at first
Then getting louder
Into a roar,
The place is a disaster.

Tosin Akande (10)
St Luke's Primary School, London

Volcano

A volcano is an angry lion,
Giant and orange, yellow and red,
His belly rumbles waiting to burst,
The rumbling, tumbling noises.

His eyes popping in and out
Looking at the smoke,
The lion roars with mighty strength
Orange, yellow and red the lava begins to boil
The lion licking his greasy, hot paws.

Pippa Thirkettle (11)
St Luke's Primary School, London

A Meteorite

A meteorite is a deadly dragon,
breathing out exhaust from its nose.
Slowly crashing to the Earth,
red, yellow and orange it flashes, *crash, bash!*

Doesn't care what people think
thinking he is the head of the world.
Lying alone worn out, after the huge fuss
He nodded off in a little shady corner.

Nana Abeyie (10)
St Luke's Primary School, London

Lightning

Lightning is
an electric eel
slithering
through the sky
with great speed
speeding through the dark
shocking enemies in
his way.

Flashing away to show
his temper
brightening up the sky
when it
strikes!

Mumin Choudouhry (11)
St Luke's Primary School, London

Tidal Wave

A tidal wave is an angry and fast-approaching hippo
It's the king of the sea
It demolishes anything that gets in its way
It crashes with all its might
It never gives up if anything stops it from charging
It's so rough it is able to knock down a building.

Sam Bassett (10)
St Luke's Primary School, London

The Rainbow

A rainbow is a colourful butterfly
Flying on top of a puffy cloud.
Shining and catching everyone's attention
It sparkles all over the land.
Fading away, after a day
The butterfly comes back another day.

With its dark and bright shades
It shines in the sky
With a great treasure no one can find
Behind the butterfly is a diamond
Each corner twinkles like a star in the summer's sun
Near the rose garden it smells the sweet smell of the summer's day.

Luisa Avery (11)
St Luke's Primary School, London

The Sea

The sea is a hungry lion
Roaring loudly and fiercely
His paws are a sharp knife
His teeth are a sharp blade
To bite his food
His fur around his head
Blowing in his face.

Stacy Humphries (10)
St Luke's Primary School, London

A Rainbow

A rainbow is a butterfly
Flapping its showy wings
Its delicate fluttering colours glittering away
It only appears on a sunny or rainy day
Children flabbergasted at the beautiful butterfly
Just look at the brightly shining wings.

Ayat Abdurahman (10)
St Luke's Primary School, London

If . . .

If my mum was a flower
She would be a beautiful lotus
Floating on the water, free
So everyone would be able to see.

If my mum was an animal,
She would be an Indian elephant,
Swaying her trunk side to side
And it would make all the animals hide.

If my mum was the sun,
She would be merry and bright,
She would come out every day,
So everyone would enjoy the light.

Bria Patel (11)
St Luke's Primary School, London

The Cloud

A cloud is a beautiful dove
Swooping merrily through the sky
With her wings floating happily by
Her pretty wings flutter in every way
Attractive and charming day by day.

And when the night falls
She would fly
Fly back to her nest way up high
Where she comes and breathes out a sigh.

Janatara Ahmed (10)
St Luke's Primary School, London

My Pop Idol

Whatever she sings comes out perfect.
I listen to her songs, it sends me to sleep.
I smell the sweetness of her voice.
She touches my heart deep inside me.
She's never bitter, always sweet.
'Pop idol,
Pop idol,
Please sign this for me.'
I picture her singing in front of me.
I see her picture in my dreams.
She sings like a bird, she howls at my moon.
Pop idol
You're the one for me
I say to myself, *you will always comfort me.*
If I had a dream it would be to see you
Just to see you
But would that come true?
My dream once again is to meet you.

Rushane McGhie (10)
Stamford Hill Primary School, London

Autumn Falls

Leaves are red and that's when they fall.
People stepping on the leaves which makes a noise.
Rain drops down like a sparkle of silver.
Children slipping and skidding around,
Having so much fun that they can't stop laughing.
I love autumn because it is a time when it's nearly winter.
I like winter because there's snow.
When there's snow there's ice.
Autumn is going but winter is coming.

Lisa Thi Tran (10)
Stamford Hill Primary School, London

Wintertime

Children running outside
Building snowmen with hats and scarves.
Adults playing with them,
Having fun with their younger ones.
Mist coming out of their mouths and red noses running.
Ice skating around, having a laugh,
With no work or school.
Just spending time with your family,
Sitting by the fire, cosy and warm,
Enjoying a cup of hot chocolate.
Youngsters who don't feel well,
Kneeling by the window watching other people,
But happy it's wintertime.

Shayo Bayo-Tofowomo (10)
Stamford Hill Primary School, London

The Way Of Nature

Sun glistening throughout the year
Birds singing beautifully
Flowers springing into bloom
Squirrels searching for their homes
Spiders weaving perfect webs
Caterpillars transforming into butterflies.

Ronell Hatto (11)
Stamford Hill Primary School, London

Seasons All Round

The flowers are blooming making beautiful sights.
Elegant flowers glow for the duration of the night.
New things are starting to grow.
Beautiful plants are beginning to show.

The feeling of the heat is somehow unusual,
But really you don't feel it at all.
Kids love the enjoyable heat,
They all say it's very neat.

The leaves that scrape on the ground,
Somehow they play a soothing sound.
Most leaves have dazzling colours that shine,
You can't tell them apart 'cause they are so fine.

The sprinkling of snow that is cold.
Lots of happy snow starts to unfold.
The kids play with the snow every day.
Keeps them happy in every way.

Raine Mondesir-Payne (11)
Stamford Hill Primary School, London

Winter Poem

Green grass like frozen webbed claws.
The grass is like ice, shining like crystal.
When you walk through the grass it makes a crunching noise.
When you feel the grass in your hand it will be like an ice block,
the ice turns into water.

Mazie Mason (11)
Stoke Community School, Rochester

School In Wintertime

It's a freezing cold day,
all the children are running
to catch the school bus.
The leaves are rustling,
they sound like the children
whining in the morning.

It is so cold,
everyone is shouting because
they can't hear each other,
as the wind is roaring so loud,
it's like a monster shouting at them.

They get on the bus,
happy to be in the warm,
the seats are as soft as cotton wool,
and they all keep warm on their journey to school.

Sophie Ross (11)
Stoke Community School, Rochester

A Winter Poem

Trees lost like lonely children.
In the frosted hills, the dust of snow,
Gleaming like a twinkling star.
The sky like glass ice.

Dean Bailey (12)
Stoke Community School, Rochester

Winter Poem

The trees are rustling their green leaves,
the pond has frozen,
you can see the reflection
of the trees.
The red ladybirds fly by,
as you see aeroplanes up so high.

A feather falls from a bird
like snow in the sky,
the wind roars like a lion in a fight,
the sky is as blue as the sea,
and the fluffy white clouds
look down on me.

Danielle Coe (9)
Stoke Community School, Rochester

The Winter Bird

The winter bird sits on a leafless tree,
like a cold statue on a leafless branch.
The winter bird tries to find a key
to a door with winter rain inside.

The person who found the key
she put it around my frosty neck for me
I used it to open the wet door
and inside more rain poured and poured
and never stopped.
And the winter bird was happy again.

Emily Williams (9)
Stoke Community School, Rochester

My Winter Poem

On this winter's day the pond is frozen,
the leaves from the trees
have fallen to the ground.
I'm watching the sun arise from its slumber
and as I watch I think of the world.

The sun has risen
the birds are awake.
I see a couple of field mice eating.
Something catches my eye,
hundreds of white puffs
running around,
for they are being chased
by a big black dog.
The dog stops
and starts panting.
Its drool drips on my head.
I run in before it gets harder.

Arri Wall (12)
Stoke Community School, Rochester

A Taste Of Life

As I sit upon the damp wood,
and I taste the fresh morning air,
I can smell the damp dirt.

I sit, I listen to the little humming
bird sing his heart out,
yet he is not heard.

I listen to the trees
swaying this way and that.

Chloe Cocker (12)
Stoke Community School, Rochester

On A Cold Winter's Day

On a cold winter's day,
the trees are bare
when the crunchy leaves
come flowing through the air.

When the leaves fall,
they come flying through my feet,
they crunch and crisp
like a sparrow's beak.

On a cold winter's night,
I can hear tapping of rain on the floor.
I put my umbrella up
but now comes more and more.

On a cold winter's day,
the trees are bare
when the crunchy leaves
come flowing through the air.

Eloise Henderson (10)
Stoke Community School, Rochester

Winter's Snow

The snow was like a big crystal ball.
There were millions and thousands
of shimmering stars.

The stars were twinkling.
Glimmering snowflakes were
as white as a polar bear's fur.

Whenever you get a piece
of snow in your hand
it will be crackling.

Leanne Button (12)
Stoke Community School, Rochester

Winter Feelings

As I walked upon the leaves outside
they smelt and felt like the crunchy nut cereal
that I had for breakfast that morning.

The grass that was upon me
was so cold that it felt
like a big bunch of snowflakes
that had just landed
with all of the others.

The fungus was so small,
that the ice had covered it
with its strong icy powers.
The fungus was smooth,
now it's hard and sharp,
like tigers' teeth.

Charles Harris (12)
Stoke Community School, Rochester

A Winter Poem

The blue sky as cold as crackling frost.
Children rolling down cold hills -
laughing and playing.
Children screaming when they have to go home.

Ashley Wall (9)
Stoke Community School, Rochester

Wildlife

Wind and leaves and stones and plants,
All sitting down on the lovely grass,
Waiting for Class 4,
Ready for the tour.

The raindrops in the air
Drip in the shape of a pear.
The clouds move down,
Like a lion, moving around.

Seeing all the willow
Scattered everywhere,
Making me get this feeling,
To clean up everywhere.

Wind and leaves and stones and plants,
All sitting down on the lovely grass,
All tired and cosy and warm,
All tucked up, safe and sound.

Tiana Kingsnorth (9)
Stoke Community School, Rochester

A Winter Poem

People running like stones
Falling to the ground,
People talking of spring,
Like the wind whistling.

Bark chippings crunching like dried leaves,
Water rippling like a pond freezing,
A door slamming like leaves rustling violently.

A rabbit leaving its burrow
Like a child leaving its house.
People going to work
Like the birds leaving their nest.

Amanda Jacobs (12)
Stoke Community School, Rochester

Winter Poem

The winter season has come,
the flowers have died
because of the cold, frosty air,
the brown, rough, crispy bark
turns into lumps of snow,
children playing in piles of leaves,
shouting and laughing with joy.

It's time to go back indoors
and time to stop playing.
It's time to go back indoors
and time to go to bed,
the children have the window open
to let the fresh air in.

It gets closer to night
and much, much colder.
Now the children know why
they have to come in,
because if they were still outside
they would be frozen and shivering.

Aimee Draper (11)
Stoke Community School, Rochester

Wintertime

The snow is like the clouds glistening
on a cold winter's day.
The leaves that fly by me rustle, like children whining.

As the snowflakes fall from the sky
they feel like they're skimming and slicing my cheek.

The wind is howling like a pack of wolves on a full moonlit night.
The snow has covered everything in sight.
I have never seen such a beautiful night.

Rebecca Gapper (10)
Stoke Community School, Rochester

My Winter Poem

The wind howls like some monster
roaring in the darkness.
I can tell it is winter
because the air is like a fan
blowing out a freezing cold breeze.

As I walk, the bark
crunches under my feet like snow.
As I feel the water from the pool
it feels like picking up a cold snowball.

As I look around I see beautiful willow sculptures
which are fragile.
As I leave I can hear the birds singing
and swaying in the trees
where the wind is blowing.

Chloe Stroud (11)
Stoke Community School, Rochester

Winter Poem

I wake one morning with a chill in the air,
I climb out of my lovely warm bed,
Then I slowly creep to my window.

I rub my eyes then I open them, to see the sun slowly rising,
And all the colours mixing together.
Then I see a thin cover of pure white over everything,
With small dots the colour of white candyfloss and the shape
of raindrops,
Falling from the sky so high.

Some children are playing outside,
Making big white snowmen and having snowball fights,
And playing on the outdoor slide.

Michelle Toland (11)
Stoke Community School, Rochester

Snowy Day

I looked out of my room
I saw the ground covered in snow.
So I went downstairs and I saw a mouse in my house
So I went out to play
and the strong wind nearly blew me over
and the Land Rover couldn't drive about.

In the snow was a toy so I looked and there it was.
I pulled it up and it was a toy car so I played with it.
My grandad came and he came with a poodle
and it was big and it kept barking all day.

Declan Kingsley (9)
Stoke Community School, Rochester

A Cold Winter's Day

Stones by the pond
and grass on the ground
the air is frozen like a polar bear's mound.

The air is cold like a big ice cube.
The leaves on the ground are
blown around like
a dead fly on the ground.
The trees in the distance are bare.
They stand like a really tall person.

Kayleigh Rousell (11)
Stoke Community School, Rochester

A Winter Poem

The heavy dark clouds like dark shadows,
With rain and snow falling from the sky,
Like dark and light wet drips falling on me,
Like lonely children,
Falling from the sky.

The heavy rain's falling down on me like
The winter's roots falling to the ground,
Like winter has planted itself to summer
With its roots round it like a mix.

Harry Hilton (10)
Stoke Community School, Rochester

Snow

Snow has come, glittering
and glistening like a crystal globe.

Snow is falling again and again,
it drops and melts.
As it settles people can see.
Be so quiet, it might come again.

Everybody listens till it drops
and makes a sound as beautiful as music.

Alice Barrett (11)
Stoke Community School, Rochester

Cloudy Sky

Cloudy sky like cotton wool,
flying across the sky,
as the wind passes by
like a little boy whistling a tune.

When the clouds go by
it looks like a metal chain,
looking like a sky-blue wall
with snowballs on it.

Feeling happy like
a baby in the snow,
smiling when the small birds
fly across.

Blair Robb (10)
Stoke Community School, Rochester

The Winter Poem

Frozen waterfall like a wall of glass.
Snow like cotton wool.
Green trees like children throwing snowballs.
Their sledges on the hills on a bend.
Minding the trees, being careful and having fun.
Some children ice skating, being safe and having fun.

Lewis Ilsley (9)
Stoke Community School, Rochester

My Winter Poem

The winter leaves are rustly,
The water freezing rapidly.
I see the whiteness of the mistletoe,
The rabbit cold in its burrow.

The Christmas food coming on fine,
My family is drinking Christmas wine.
I hear the mighty roar of the wind,
The snow is falling on my chin.

The fungus is as black as pewter,
People banging on a fence.
The frosty bark crunches as I tread,
And the birds have been fed.

James Blown (11)
Stoke Community School, Rochester

Wildlife

Frogs in the pond,
stones on the ground,
waiting for the warm to come round.

The water is as cold as ice
and it is as silent as mice.
And you can hear raindrops
dropping on the ice.
A cold swimming pool
is just as nice.

Sean Turner (9)
Stoke Community School, Rochester

Winter Has Come

Drifting snow has come
Across our town
Icicles are made
But where is the sound?

Mist has come all in peace
Bitter winds blowing east
Snowflakes falling everywhere
I am cold, do you have a blanket to spare?

Making snowmen in the snow
It is fun, do you know?

Making snowmen, round and fat
I sit on an ice-cold mat
Frosty cold and glistening grass
Blizzards are coming now and then.

Looking up to the frozen sky
Seeing glistening stars
Wanting to walk on nice, cold Mars
Telling my mum I'm going out, what a lie!

Frozen lake, what a sight
Sparkling all night
Will it break
Or will it not, who knows?

But soon spring will come
And look, it's here!

Bethany Martin (9)
West Borough Primary School, Maidstone

Winter Eyes

Drifting snowflakes all around,
People skating on the ice.
Shining snowflakes they look so nice,
Bits of ice floating on the lake,
A crisp wind in my hair,
Waiting at the windowpane,
Snow drifting far, far away,
I see no people about.
All of a sudden I thought my eyes were playing a trick on me,
I saw the last drop of snow,
Winter is over, spring has begun,
No more gloomy nights.

Ashleigh Briggs (9)
West Borough Primary School, Maidstone

Wintertime

Sparkling snow in the night
Frozen ice on my house
Shining stars in the sky
Cold so intense, so deep, so still

People playing in the darkness
Fog and dark in the world
Snowmen smiling round the street
Winter's coming to our world.

Darshna Rajesh Nemane (10)
West Borough Primary School, Maidstone

I Can See

I can see icy rains,
Dripping down the windowpane.
I can see people skating on ice,
It looks cold but very nice.
I can see slippery streets,
And people falling off their feet.
I can see friend and foe,
Playing in the pure white snow.
I can see icicles glistening,
Feel and hear the winter winds whispering.
I can see someone on a sledge,
Oh no, he is going to crash into the hedge!

Summer Leagas (9)
West Borough Primary School, Maidstone

Winter Begins

Moaning, howling, drifting wind,
Means the season winter begins,
Glistening, glittering, shining mist,
Means the season winter exists,
Draughty, darkness, blizzards dim,
Hear the carol singers sing,
Frozen, frosty, bitter rain,
Dripping on the windowpane,
Hear the sound of the north wind blow,
Blowing through the falling snow.

Rianne Hobbs (10)
West Borough Primary School, Maidstone

Winter's Beginning

Drifting snow,
Bitter wind,
Mist everywhere,
Sun shining through,

Icicles hang,
Snowflakes fall,
Cloudy mist through and through,
Slippery ice,

Glimmering snow,
Glistening glow,
Glittering icicles,

Sparkling snowmen,
Frozen feet,
People slipping in the street,

Blanket of snow on the ground,
My bedroom curtains are pulled,
As winter begins.

Jodie Hall (10)
West Borough Primary School, Maidstone

Winter

W inter snow, falling, falling,
I cy wind, whistling, blowing,
N ot a place without snow,
T rees whistling with wind blowing,
E veryone's waiting for,
R obin's call.

Betony Dubock (8)
West Borough Primary School, Maidstone

Falling Snowflakes

The snow is great
Snowmen standing
Boys and girls making snowmen
Children making snow angels
People running round and round in circles
People are having fun
Clouds as white as ever
The sun is not out
Everyone is playing, playing in the snow
It is snowing, snowing forever!
People going out to town
It is fun.

Ryan Noon (9)
West Borough Primary School, Maidstone

Winter Wonderland

Winter is white,
And is such a pretty sight,
Coffee in the morning,
As the day is dawning,
Ice is on the ground,
And the snowmen are around.

Charlotte Livingstone (11)
West Borough Primary School, Maidstone

A Park Of Snow

Walking through a park of snow,
Looking at the sky,
Admiring the frosted rings,
Which I see glinting with my eyes.

Gazing at a blanket of snow,
It looks white and sleet,
Freshly laid with love and care,
Try not to ruin it with my feet.

Now the sun is coming out,
No one wants to cheer,
As the snow is going to melt,
We'll have to wait till next year.

Rosie Judge (11)
West Borough Primary School, Maidstone

Gods And Goddesses

Gods and goddesses of ancient Greece
Some are kind and some are sweet
They will help us through the day
Every single step of the way,
            Hey!

He's called Zeus and he's called Hades
And some of them are even ladies
They will help us through the day
Every single step of the way
            Hey!

Bryony Curtis (8)
West Borough Primary School, Maidstone

Starry Night

I looked up at the sky on a
starry night,
The stars were dark, the moon
was bright,
Then all of a sudden I heard
someone shout,
'Are there any clouds about?'
'No!' I answered back
with glee,
'Not any that I can see!'
Then I noticed it started
to rain,
Oh, how that was a pain!

Kathleen Boakes (11)
West Borough Primary School, Maidstone

Claret And Blue
(The West Ham United bus)

I'm a true claret and blue
'Cause the main thing I do
Is watch West Ham's football games
While on my PS2.
I got so annoyed when the Hammers
Were screwed of the final
Of the play-offs against the
Non-true red and blue
Stupid Crystal Palace. *Boo!*

Mark Skinner (11)
West Borough Primary School, Maidstone

Winter

W inter is near.
I cicles clear,
N ight so bright,
T he coldest season of the year.
E very child dresses warm,
R eady to play out in the snow.

Hayley Nyman (8)
West Borough Primary School, Maidstone

Winter Poem

W inter is cold
I ce is frozen
N ests are built in a barn
T rees are bare
E veryone is wrapped up warm
R obins chirp for winter.

Kimberley Grace Mercer (9)
West Borough Primary School, Maidstone

Winter

W inter
I s here, the
N ight is clear
T he coldest season has now arrived.
E very child dressed up warm
R eady to go out and play snowballs.

Tom Tucker (8)
West Borough Primary School, Maidstone

The Highwaymen

Down the snow-capped lane,
Came two highwaymen!
Both on pitch-black stallions,
They were wearing some gems!
They walked to my old cottage door,
My heart pounded more and more,
I grabbed a stick,
Went to the door . . .
And *whip!*
They disappeared on a trip!

Jade Bunyan-Wilding (11)
West Borough Primary School, Maidstone

Liverpool

Liverpool are so cool.
They're the masters of football.
Liverpool also rule,
Except when they're not feeling quite so perky,
It's because they've eaten too much turkey!

Bradley J Marchant (10)
West Borough Primary School, Maidstone

Winter Poem

Winter is cold, frosty and misty
Snowmen stand, full of pride
Sleet forms icicles, rain forms snow
Lapland is fun as we are skating
Children at school, stuck inside
December has blizzards full of ice.

Zoe Smith (11)
West Borough Primary School, Maidstone

The Shadow In The Moonlight

Soft and quiet the paw does pound,
Running swiftly on the ground.
The shadow follows the light of the moon,
Hoping to get to the surrounding soon.

Breathing heavily the creature flies by,
Not going to make it but must try.
Home before dawn, the shadow does moan,
Get there to claim the sky for my own.

Running, running, must get there soon,
To show that I live in the light of the moon.
Top of the mountain the creature growls,
Lifts its head up into the moonlight and . . .

Howls!

Eden Selway (11)
West Borough Primary School, Maidstone

Animals Look Like Things!

An elephant looks like a big bouncy ball.
A furry lion looks like a nice cosy bed.
A fast tortoise looks like a patterned stone
And a butterfly looks like a fairy, yes, a fairy!

Ella Selway (7)
West Borough Primary School, Maidstone

My Rabbit

My lovely rabbit is like a wonderful daughter,
She is like a sweet and kind mare,
She is a brown and white darling,
My family and I love her as much as she loves us.

Louise Paine (8)
West Borough Primary School, Maidstone

Snowy Times

Clouds drift away in the sky,
Snow falling from the sky, fly.
Icicles drip gradually onto the ground,
And they never make a sound.

Snowflakes all wet and cold,
But they never make a sound.
The glistening rivers run,
And it's always lots of fun.

Snow angels shaped on the snow,
And we never ever know.
Snowmen made upright,
Some made down low.

Fog appears over the hills,
And then my friend comes, Sahil.
Trees are frozen from standing in the cold,
Apples are covered in mould.

Emilia Page (9)
West Borough Primary School, Maidstone

Anger

Anger is the colour red
It smells of steam
Anger tastes of burnt bacon
It sounds like teeth scraping together.
Anger lives in death.

Maxwell Whiting (9)
West Borough Primary School, Maidstone

Joey

My name is Joey,
I'm a kangaroo,
I live in Australia,
How about you?

I have a tail
And a furry pouch,
My great big feet
Don't fit on the couch

I have a friend
Called Koala Ken,
I'll see you soon
But I don't know when!

Hannah Daly (9)
West Borough Primary School, Maidstone

Winter

W hooshing snowballs through the air,
 I t's the coldest season here,
N othing is the same,
T reacherous roads and slippery ice,
E veryone is wrapped up warm,
R eady to go and play in the snow.

Luke Osina (9)
West Borough Primary School, Maidstone

Winter Snow

Snowflakes drifting down to the ground,
Blizzards so rough you cannot walk,
Icicles hanging down from the roof,
Snow angels have been covered over.

Children running out to play,
Snow angels, snowmen, all being made,
Adults skating on the ice,
Snow looks so bright.

Snowflakes glistening as they fall,
A frozen lake,
It's going to break!
The shining lake is so bright.

Lucy Kelly (10)
West Borough Primary School, Maidstone

Winter Wonderland

Icicles are hung
Winter's begun
Blizzards are blowing
The deepness is growing
Sleet is falling
Frost is calling
Marshmallows are roasting
The fire is toasting.

Miriam Lebrette (11)
West Borough Primary School, Maidstone

Snow Song

Winter is white and full of joys,
And snowball fights will happen between the boys.
People are slipping and skidding,
While other people are having fun sledging.

In the north there is always snow,
But down south, you never know.
Some people are wearing jumpers,
But T-shirt people are really bonkers.

Marcus Edwards (10)
West Borough Primary School, Maidstone

Snow

Snow, snow, playing with the wind
Snow looking fluffy and white
Making snowmen and snow angels
Snowflakes falling from the sky.

Making footprints through the snow
Fluffy snowballs and snow is squashy
Snow is very deep and soft
Snow is fun to play in but very crunchy.

Geetha Thaninathan (9)
West Borough Primary School, Maidstone

All About Me And My Pets

My flowing hair looks like a shiny sparkler.
My amazing hair looks like a furry slipper.
My thin hair looks like some slimy snakes.
My cute puppy looks like a fluffy pillow.

Lacie Shepherd (8)
West Borough Primary School, Maidstone

Snow!

Snow is fluffy,
Snow is white,
Everybody loves a snowball fight!
When it's cold all the adults say,
'Don't worry children, go and play!'
We run about and play all day,
It is very chilly but we're OK!
This is for you to remember,
On this cold winter's day!

Kaye-Dee Evanson (11)
West Borough Primary School, Maidstone

My Hair is Like . . .

My hair is like . . .
a teddy bear when you cuddle him on the bed.

My hair is coloured like . . .
autumn leaves.

It is like . . .
a gold curtain moving in the breeze.

Martha La Rosa-Butler (7)
West Borough Primary School, Maidstone

Being On An Island

This tiny island is like a boiling oven
That minute sandpit is like this sandy desert.
The burning sun is like a flaming fireball coming to get us . . . *help!*
That school of glistening fish is like a colossal whale
. . . *Wow!*

Joe Dolan (7)
West Borough Primary School, Maidstone

Sunny Days

The sun is bright and beautiful,
it doesn't look like rain.
It's as golden as the goldest part of the sand,
it keeps me warm on cold days.

The sun destroys the thunder and keeps me warm again,
it's as round as a beach ball,
as bright as a sunflower.
But when it's time for the sun to go,
I say goodbye for another day.

Aaron Challis (9)
West Borough Primary School, Maidstone

Me And My Body

My glowing eyes look like some flashing traffic lights!
My wide open mouth is like a long door opening.
My hairy legs look like a prickly tree!
My fat belly likes eating delicious cakes!
My greedy hands are like a petrol pump sticking fuel in a car.

Ashley Witham (8)
West Borough Primary School, Maidstone

The Snow Poem

When there's snow outside
Children go and hide.
When Frosty's out to play
The children cheer, 'Hip hip hooray!'
When the icicles drop,
My grandma knits a woolly top.

Luke Collins (11)
West Borough Primary School, Maidstone

Snow Fun

Snow here, snow there, snow everywhere,
I'm here, snow's there, can't go anywhere
Stuck at home, being bored, can't do anything . . .

Tricked my mum, went outside and had lots and lots of fun.
Made snowmen, made snow girls, that night
Threw snowballs at my friends and did some more, that's right!
I ice-skated, snowboarded and bashed into a fence,
Had some ice cream, froze to death.
Said 'Goodbye,' and went home to bed!

Raha Choudhury (8)
West Borough Primary School, Maidstone

Squashed Oranges

Oranges are round
Oranges are sweet
Oranges smell very weird
Just like your size 11 feet.

Oranges are round
Oranges are fat
But when you run them over
They make a loud *splat!*

Sam Brookes (11)
West Borough Primary School, Maidstone

Winter Wonderland

Bitter and cold winds
Sweep the land.
The icicles so sharp and spiky.
Clouds form in the darkening sky.
Grit is laid on the ground
To spoil the fun.

The snowmen are melting down to the ground,
That means winter is nearly over.
Soon it's spring, with no snow.
Now I can't make snow angels, snowmen,
And throw snowballs.
I hate spring, I like winter.

Ryan Richard West (9)
West Borough Primary School, Maidstone

Winter, Winter

Winter, winter, is so cold.
I can't stand it, I don't like cold.

Winter, winter, we all catch a cold.
I like staying in bed all the time.

Winter, winter, wrap up warm.
If you don't, you will get ill.

Winter, winter, is so cold!
I can't bear it anymore
And I wish I could cuddle a teddy bear.

Phoebe Mitchell (8)
West Borough Primary School, Maidstone

Winter

The snow is falling thick and fast,
It's covered all the trees and grass,
The roofs of houses are all white,
Everywhere looks clean and bright.

Robins high up in the trees,
Singing songs so merrily,
Snowmen standing tall and bold,
Children's hands and feet so cold.

Snowballs flying through the air,
Children playing without a care,
They went outside and played in the snow,
Even though their mums said, 'No!'

Paul Fisher (9)
West Borough Primary School, Maidstone

Happiness

Happiness is warm like a summer's morning.
Happiness smells like a cake being baked.
Happiness feels like a waterbed.
Happiness sounds like a bird singing.
Happiness tastes like an ice cream.
Happiness lives in your heart.

Ricky Fellowes (9)
West Borough Primary School, Maidstone

Winter Weather

Crisp snow on the ground,
Snowmen dripping all around,
Winds blow, cold and damp,
Children running, running, *clank,*

Icicles sitting on blanket-covered houses,
People cold in thin white blouses,
Everyone sitting in their homes,
Warm by the fire even when they're eating ice cream cones,

Frosty skies up above,
Children giving each other a shove,
Glistening snowflakes in the mist,
Hot Christmas pudding, oh what bliss!

Ice-skating in a ring,
Snowboarding while the blackbirds sing.

Hannah Pearson (9)
West Borough Primary School, Maidstone

Winter's Snow

Everyone's wrapped up warm,
When the blizzards form.
Children are making snow angels,
Oh, it's very cold today.

Sparkling snowflakes silently fall,
Icicles hang from trees and gutters,
Now the bitter winds blow.

Lauren Mounteney (9)
West Borough Primary School, Maidstone

Winter

The howling winds of winter blow.
Blow away all this freezing snow.
I'm stuck inside playing Chequers all day.
Please rain, try to wash this snow away.
I can't go outside, there's so much snow.
Wash it away so I can go
And play with my friends in sun, not snow.
Not in this wet, snowy place full of darkness,
But a sunny, springy place of happiness.

James Weaver (9)
West Borough Primary School, Maidstone

A Snowy Day

It's a snowy day,
It's time to play,
Santa rides around to play
In his supersonic sleigh.

Skidding on ice,
Sounds quite nice.
Big snow piles are very deep,
But now it's time to go to sleep.

Kahlil Socobos (9)
West Borough Primary School, Maidstone

Winter, Winter

Winter, winter, really fun
there's no sun in winter,
but you can have fun,
there's snow to throw,
you can play all day,
because it is snowing!

Nathan Kury (7)
West Borough Primary School, Maidstone

Snow Poem

Snow is white and fluffy
and is soft and furry.
When I walk on the snow
it crunches and glows.
Sometimes when I sleigh down,
I go whizzing past the trees,
Faster and faster . . .
I never know when to stop!

Dylan Stallard (8)
West Borough Primary School, Maidstone

Winter, Winter

Winter, winter, winter, it is very nice.
On your little nose it feels like ice.
When sitting on a bench
You can feel the frost and cold.
It can turn you silly,
Then you will not be told.

Alex Warner (8)
West Borough Primary School, Maidstone